W9-BNE-998

The first Atomic Bomb Peace Picture

was produced by a boy's school. They had help from an alumnus, Orson Welles, and an opening night in New York's Museum of Modern Art. An audience of distinguished guests were gathered there and amazing things happened. A British M.P. asked for a print. It became the first movie ever to be shown in the Houses of Parliament. Eleanor Roosevelt had UNESCO buy twenty prints and show them all over the world. Because the Welles name was involved, most of our colleges rented the picture. The program passed out in New York had this heading:

Rip Van Winkle Renascent

This is a 16mm, Kodachrome allegory in swing-time. But despite its syncopation and its raucous satire, the authors are deadly serious. We almost called it

A SERMON ON A MOUNT

The picture was written and produced by

THE TODD SCHOOL at WOODSTOCK, ILLINOIS

.... Cast of Characters ....
.... See Present Page 32 ....

This Script of the first anti-nuclear Movie
is published by the
HORTENSE GETTYS HILL MEMORIAL FUND FOR PEACE
Box 2153, Rockford, IL 61130

The book, ISBN 0-9613799-0-1 $4.60
Videotape of the film, VHS or Beta $20.00

CONTENTS

Forty pages of atomic history precede this script of the first anti-nuclear movie. These pages are not organized into definitive chapters. Instead, you will find rambling recollections of a nonagenarian deeply involved with nuclear matters since 1939. These involvements include:

1. The Manhattan Project. This huge effort built our bomb and saved our Free World. It was triggered by Einstein's letter to Roosevelt warning that Hitler's laboratories were close to producing the ultimate weapon. Fortunately, Europe's foremost atomic scientists had fled the continent and were teaching in America. These were marshaled into the great Project which had two locations. One was in Oak Ridge, Tennessee; the other in a huge laboratory covering miles of dessert near Los Alamos, New Mexico. Our son had a minor position in Oak Ridge; my cousin, a major one in Los Alamos. To produce an atomic bomb, radio-active plutonium was necessary. This was extracted from uranium ore using the huge power available from TVA dams. The fissionable product was shipped to Los Alamos. There, in three years of super-secret labor, a dozen men of genius, assisted by 5000 lesser scientists, won the race that saved our world from a madman's *Thousand-Year Reich.* Joe McGinniss, whose books have all been best sellers, is writing one on Los Alamos. He calls it *The Forbidden City.* This is history that calls out for documentation. The fate of the world hung on the work expended there. That was only forty years ago and yet the story is fading from memory.

2. Robert Wilson. A biography. This is the foremost living atomic scientist. He happens to be my young cousin; young compared to my 90 years. At 10, in our Todd School, he was nicknamed *The Inventor.* In college, at Berkely, he was a protege of the great Ernest O. Lawrence who had just won a Nobel prize for inventing the cyclotron. So our boy, when a mere undergraduate, worked with that first atom-smashing instrument and was an assistant to its inventor. With his doctorate, he was called to Princeton to head a team studying the atom. For the Manhattan Project, he brought his team to Los Alamos and became head of nuclear physics research. *At the age of 29!*

Later, our *Atomic Energy Commission* chose Wilson to design and build the largest atom-smasher in the world, The *Fermi National Acceleration Laboratory.* This sprawls across 6,800 square miles of Illinois prairie 35 miles west of Chicago. Huge buildings of Bob's innovative design control the heart of the project, a buried 4-mile ring of machinery that pushes protons up to 99.99 percent of the speed of light. He resigned as Director recently and now spends most of his time lecturing to fellow scientists around the world. A fairly complete biography of this dichotomous man who is both bomb builder and pacifist; both scientist and artist, starts on page 9.

3. The Hills in Hiroshima. America's feeling of guilt over the suffering of survivors led to the establishment of the *Atomic Bomb Casualty Commission.* They chose a friend of ours, an anthropoligist from Antioch College, Dr. Earle Reynolds, to head a study of radiation damage. Until he and his wife, Barbara, could establish a home in Hiroshima, they brought their son, Tim, to our Todd School. When Earle saw pictures of two schooners on a wall, the conversation shifted from Tim's curriculum to the father's addiction to the sea. The scientist who labored in a laboratory had never lived near an ocean. But he had read the Joshua Slocum classic, *Sailing Alone Around the World* and never lost a desire to duplicate that feat. I said the desire should now be a possibility. He was headed for a seaport that would surely have a shipyard and probably cheap labor. We spent an hour telling of our ocean sailing and discussing the best type of deep-sea rig. Three years later, after Earle's casualty work was complete, the family set out in his 50-foot ketch, *Phoenix,* for a journey around the world.

His wife, Barbara, is the most amazing woman the Hills have ever met. She established the *World Friendship Center* in Hiroshima and through it we had the privilege of living in the home of survivors. The tatami mats were not too uncomfortable but wooden pillows had to be discarded in favor of folded clothing. Bathing was in a communal bathhouse where we showered, rinsed, and then inched our way down into steaming water. The trick is not to agitate it. This makes it unbearable. Our departure was touching. The formal bows on arrival now became embraces. These for Americans who had killed their children and left them suffering with leukemia and cancer. Their forgiveness was not a tribute to us but to our friend, Barbara-san. That suffix is one of endearment.

4. Movie Making. We are bombarded with questions on how this film was produced. An army of young moderns who now own video cameras hope to use these creatively. Many schools and most universities offer credit courses in "Cinema". Text books on the subject abound. This 20-page section is not another. Instead, it is a look into the long ago when the Todd School first made movies. Color film had not been invented. All pictures were silent. Orson Welles was deeply involved. A lifetime partnership began. Shakespeare texts we collaborated on when he was a boy have broken all sales records. If the amazing story of the Welles childhood interests you, turn to page 67.

Mail Orders
Your book store may not stock videotapes. They are available from the
Hortense Hill Fund
Box 2153, Rockford, IL 61130
Orders will be filled the day your check is received.
Here are prices which include transportation:
A videotape, VHS or Beta, $22.00
A Peace Group package consisting of 30 books and one tape is $85.00.
Add tax where applicable.
The phone number of the Fund is 815/963-0358
When our office is empty, you will be asked to leave a message on a tape.
If it needs an answer you will get one on the phone or in the mail.
If you are simply curious about our activities, here is a summary:

The fund is organized as a corporation which helps the favorite charities of Hortense. These include all of the groups actively working for peace. Oldest of these is the *American Friends Service Committee,* the Quaker group that led us to Hiroshima. Dozens of others are listed in the Grove Press Handbook, "Stop Nuclear War". Our cousin, Robert Wilson, founded the first one called *Federation of American Scientists,* referred to as "the conscience of the physicists". Then there's Horty's favorite domestic charity, *The Salvation Army.* And many others.

The Door that Closed Forever

On the night of July 16, 1945, the foremost scientists in the world, many of them Nobel prize winners, were sleeping under the stars on the sands of the Alamagordo desert. Twenty miles away, atop a steel tower, was a weapon they had designed and built during three years of frantic effort and super secrecy in Los Alamos. Its test would come just before dawn. They were warned to keep heads down and eyes averted during the initial blast. When it was safe to look up they beheld a mushroom of fire that filled the sky. It was a door that closed forever on our past.

The door that shuts us out also shuts us in. Facing a future that is ominous. First there was hope of a brave new world. It would be filled with free energy. Hunger would be eliminated. There was water under the deserts. Just lift it up and Isaiah's prophesy would come true. They would now blossom like the rose. Alas, that water has yet to be lifted. Nuclear generators proved fantastically expensive. Then Three-Mile-Island proved them potentially dangerous. Now we know our immediate danger is minor compared to the coming danger to our descendants. Safe disposal of atomic waste is impossible. It must go into our land, our water or, by burning, into our air. Any of these alternatives leave a time-bomb ticking for the product of our loins. On top of these hazards, we still have politicians who talk of **winning** an atomic war. **"Whom the gods would destroy, they first make mad."**

Speaking of madness, we now learn that thousands in the nuclear program have been removed from responsibility because of "mental disorders". The Defense Department has a *Personnel Reliability Program.* This to screen out undesirables. A House subcommittee has reported that in one year, 1219 nuclear personnel had to be removed from duty because of mental trauma, 1365 for abuse of drugs and 256 for alcoholism. An officer in a missile silo wrote of his underground job in *Air Force* magazine: "There is no entertainment to pass the time and relieve the monotony. A crew member tries not to think about his ultimate responsibility which could lead to the killing of millions of people. He becomes schizoid.' Well he might . As **launch officer** it will be his finger that pressses the final awesome button. He needs a higher authority plus a coded release to do this. That final mistake has not yet occured but given the odds and Murphy's Law and the fallibility of man and his machines, it's only a matter of time.

If we won't listen to our scientists and our philosophers, listen to our soldiers:

Dwight Eisenhower says:

In any outbreak of general hostilities destruction will be both reciprocal and complete. The era of armaments has ended. The human race must conform to this truth or die.

Douglas MacArthur says:

Men like me are now obsolete. There can be no more great wars. The term "Nuclear-war" is self-deluding. A war has victors. Nuclear-war has only victims. It is planetary suicide.

On the next page listen to our philosophers

4

Tennyson's Amazing Prophesy

One hundred and forty-two years ago Lord Tennyson looked up at the sky in his Locksley Hall and had a vision. With a quill pen he started to write his amazing prophesy:

For I dipped into the future far as human eye could see,
Saw a vision of the world and all the wonders that would be.

Eighty-one years before the Wright Brothers struggled their bamboo contraption off the ground at Kitty Hawk, the prophet wrote:

Saw the heavens filled with commerce, argosies of magic sails,
Pilots of the purple twilight dropping down with costly bales.

Fifty-nine years before Billy Mitchell was court marshalled by fellow officers in the Navy for stating that bombs in an airplane could cause more grief to an enemy than cannons on a ship's deck, Tennyson wrote:

Heard the heavens filled with shouting and there rain'd a ghastly dew
From the nation's airy navies grappling in the central blue;

But his final couplets fortelling a World Federation remain only an inspired hope. Wilson's League and our own U.N. have been tried and found wanting.

Then the war-drums beat no longer and the battle flags were furled
In the Parliment of Man, the Federation of the World.

There the common sense of most did hold a fretful world in awe
And the kindly earth did prosper lapped in universal law.

That Parliment of Man is still in the future but not an impossible dream. The **World Federalist Association** is now funded and operating. Their phone and their address is listed in every large city directory. Get their litature and join the ranks. They surely have a long road ahead of them but just as surely they are making progress toward the difficult Tennyson dream.

As **Rip**, the Common Man in our play says: **But we're not ready for it.** As **Van Bummel,** his mentor says: *Of course we're not ready for it but there's no other way out. It's either that or extinction.*

Four decades have passed and it now looks as if we may choose extinction!

FORTY YEARS OF NUCLEAR HISTORY
A Foreward by Roger Hill

This was the first anti-nuclear film. It was produced a few months after that death cloud rose over Hiroshima. It met with instant success starting with an opening night in New York's Museum of Modern Art. Then it was screened in most American colleges and distributed world-wide by UNESCO. A print of that 45-minute movie cost hundreds of dollars and had to be rented for thirty. Now a videotape is being **sold** *for* **twenty**. If not available in your bookstore, write to the

HORTENSE GETTYS HILL MEMORIAL FUND FOR PEACE
located in Rockford, III.
Box 2153, Zip 61130
Phone, 815-963-0358

Hortense, the amazing activist known as "Horty" to thousands of devotees from Hollywood to Hiroshima, died recently at 87. She was a friend of Eleanor Roosevelt and they shared platforms during the early Peace Movement. Each was a delegate to the San Francisco Conference that produced the Charter of the United Nations.

A Memorial was held for the gorgeous gal. It was a celebration rather than a lamentation. More laughter than tears. Orson Welles closed his tribute with:

―――――――――

"Of everyone I've known, she was the most truly **passionate**. *Yes, passionate in every good meaning of a word I choose with care. Other great and good souls may be described as "warm" or warmhearted. That's too tepid sounding for Hortense. Warm is a word for comfort and consolation. The word for her was Heat.* **Fire**. *The very element itself."*

―――――――――

I'm the surviving partner of Hortense. We were married in college 68 years ago. For most of those decades we operated the off-beat Todd School at Woodstock, Illinois, where boys preparing for college would also prepare for careers. This by operating businesses as diverse as a dairy farm, a publishing company, an airport, a traveling theater and a movie studio.

Before the bomb at Hiroshima we produced a stage play that used the **Rip** theme. It had no climax but was a political satire in three acts covering three decades: the 20's, 30's and early 40's. We made **Rip** the American voter in a tricorn hat. Also in drowsy isolation up there on a mountain. His Mentor and sometime companion was **Derrick Van Bummel,** Washington Irving's school teacher turned into a timeless immortal who had endured since Bunker Hill and now was **Uncle Sam** incarnate. These two could see our globe floating beneath them. They described and discussed the changing scene in America during three decades. First it was the 1920's filled with **flappers, gangsters,** and **coonskin-coated** collegians.

> (Note: Those were the wild and wacky "ballyhoo years" recalled in Frederick Allen's epic 1931 masterpiece "Only Yesterday." If you've never read this, hurry to your library or book store. It's a classic. It has never been out of print and is now available in paperback. It tells thousands of facts and foibles, both tragic and funny, of a unique era. It details the presidency of that pitiful little politician, Warren G. Harding from the criminality of his cabinet to the sordidness of his personal life which included copulations with Nat Britton in a White House coat-closet. To this day it is unclear whether he committed suicide because he was about to be discovered in connivance with Secretary Fall and all the rest in the Teapot Dome robbery or whether his wife murdered him. He died from a "heart attack" while alone with her in Alaska.

Next came the **30's** when the mountaineers looked down on the **stock market crash** and **apple selling** on street corners. In the **40's** it was the rise of **Hitlerism** and the **Pearl Harbor** debacle. Then more American disaster until the battle of **Midway** and the Japanese retreat into the Solomons. The war was still in progress but victory was in sight. Hitler was retreating to the Rhine and Yamamoto was backed into the Solomons. Headlines still shouted news of the war but America was looking ahead and editorial pages were filled with plans for the future.

We belonged to an organization called **The Committee to Insure a Just Peace** *and in September of '43 shared a Chicago Platform with the principal speakers,* **Orson Welles** *and* **Paul Robeson.** *The night before, in a hotel room, Orson penciled his talk and I typed it. I still have that original. It included this paragraph:*

> "Dinosaurs of reaction will print it in their newspapers that I am a communist. Communists know better. I am an overpaid movie producer with pleasant reasons to rejoice— and I do— in the wholesome practicability of the profit system. I'm all for making money if it means earning it. But surely my right to having more than enough is cancelled if I don't use that more to help those that have less. This sense of Humanity's interdependence antidates Karl Marx."

The **Rip** stage play then being presented by the **Todd Troupers** had no climax but its political satire was praised by critics as being "socially significant" and we planned to put it on film where we could use news-reel clips and **show** Hitler's rise and the Japanese triumphs instead of just hearing them described by men on a mountain.

Then Hiroshima!!! Now the political allegory that lacked a climax had the greatest one in history. We added the death cloud and extra puppet scenes where **Wotan, Thor, and Mars** *rejoice in their warrior's heaven with such chants as* **Forget your qualms / With atom bombs / Now we can crack the stars.** *From their miracle mountain* **Rip** *and* **Bummel** *look down on a world in flames. From up there the skeptic and the idealist debate the future. They finally agree that the one hope left is Tennyson's dream.*

The bomb was dropped August 5th when Todd was filled with college students. We used the campus in the summer for peace activities. During the war our State Department had given college scholarships to brilliant young folks from abroad: Europe, Africa, Saudie Arabia, Iraq, Iran, and India. In the winters they learned about America — our mores and politics. In the summers they learned about each other, their *home lands and politics. They were attending a **Todd International Seminar** conducted by the **American Friends Service Committee,** activist arm of the **Quakers.** Leading political Scientists came to live with them, listen to them, and counsel them.*

We become involved with Hiroshima

That summertime involvement with the Quakers led to our close association with Hiroshima later. But all of that was *after* the bomb. To keep this story in sequence I'll go back to Los Alamos; back to the frantic race with Hitler to build a super weapon. His scientists knew that nuclear fission was possible. Their problem was to control it. America's supreme good fortune was that Germany had banished Einstein. Until 1933 he was head of the *Kaiser Wilhelm Physical Institute* in Berlin. Then he left for a few days to lecture in England. While away, Hitler, the anti-Jew, confiscated his property and revoked his German citizenship. A dozen countries offered posts to the great man. He chose America and, until his death in 1955, headed Princeton's *Institute of Advanced Studies.* In 1939 he wrote Roosevelt the famous letter that triggered the **Manhattan Project** which saved our world from a madman's "Thousand-Year-Reich".

Under Robert Oppenheimer, 4,500 of the free world's finest scientist were assembled in super-secrecy and then isolated for three years in a huge desert laboratory at Los Alamos. There they designed and built the world's first atomic bomb. Oppenheimer chose a young cousin of mine, Robert Wilson, to head his crucial department, *Nuclear Physics Research.* Bob was only 29 but had been amazingly mature since childhood. When 10, his parents were getting a divorce and he spent a year at Todd, our unique school where boys operated their own dairy farm and other businesses. His classmates nicknamed him *The Inventor* because of contraptions he built out of erector sets and the gadgets he made in the school shops.

Then an uncle, Elmer Rathbun, with a ranch in Wyoming, arranged for him to come there and his Todd-type education continued. Which means that he was given *responsibility.* At 12 he would spend weeks alone in the mountains riding herd. There was a bunk in his small cabin and a bed-roll for nights on the range. At 13 he was a competent blacksmith making parts for machinery that broke down and inventing machinery for stacking hay. Some boy! Self-reliant. Capable. Imaginative. Small wonder that when he got to college in Berkeley the great Ernest Lawrence made him his protege. Lawrence had just won the Nobel prize for inventing the cyclotron and Bob, as a mere undergraduate, worked with that first atom-smashing instrument and as an assistant to its inventor. Starting with that tiny tool, he was to become the world's foremost authority on accelerators and be chosen by our Atomic Energy Commission to design and build the largest one in the world.

Much has been written about this amazing and dichotomous man who is both bomb builder and pacifist; both scientist and artist. His sculptures range from marble to wood and from abstracts to nudes. Examples adorn our cities and our campuses. This is a **Renaissance Man** *but living in our 20th century. As for his huge new triumph at the NAL — Fermi National Accelerator Laboratory — much has been written and I'll give some excerpts. The* **Wall Street Journal** *ended an article on its value for science with these paragraphs about the director as an artist and an architect.*

Robert Wilson seized control of Fermilab from the architectural engineers right from the start and knocked $100 million off their original $350 million cost projection. He then proceeded to build his gorgeous lab for a few million less than the $250 million appropriated by Congress in 1969. Mr. Wilson had seen a picture of the Ford Foundation Building in New York and admired the open, tree-filled space that runs up the center from ground level to the top floor. Thus inspired, Mr. Wilson went on to build a more interesting, much cheaper, far more human space for his central laboratory building. Where the Ford building is formal and cold, Mr. Wilson's prairie skyscraper has a cafeteria spilling out into the lobby. "I was worried about people communicating," he recalls. "I put the restaurant downstairs, instead of upstairs, so that everyone would have to go through the same place. You can see everyone while you're waiting for the elevator."

He wanted openness, which he achieved with two glass walls at the front and back of the building, the open atrium and its two side walls, which are a pair of unenclosed monolithic stairs. Because the working part of the laboratory is entirely closed off from the central atrium and the giant staircases, this enormous space qualified as a legal fire stairway, without any of the claustrophobic ugliness such places have in other buildings.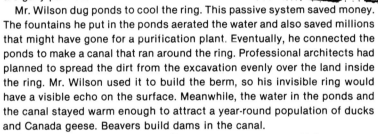

Outlying buildings had to be put together cheaply, but Mr. Wilson livened them up and unified an otherwise scattered and drab site with primary colors and supergraphic suns and moons. The magnets in the underground ring, which almost no one ever sees, are painted in bright colors that correspond to their functions but also turn a four-mile burrow into a colossal drama of gently curving hues. Even plumbing pipes in bathrooms, miles from the central lab, are gaily painted.

Mr. Wilson dug ponds to cool the ring. This passive system saved money. The fountains he put in the ponds aerated the water and also saved millions that might have gone for a purification plant. Eventually, he connected the ponds to make a canal that ran around the ring. Professional architects had planned to spread the dirt from the excavation evenly over the land inside the ring. Mr. Wilson used it to build the berm, so his invisible ring would have a visible echo on the surface. Meanwhile, the water in the ponds and the canal stayed warm enough to attract a year-round population of ducks and Canada geese. Beavers build dams in the canal.

Mr. Wilson did so many things, sly and useful and pretty, hiding a pumping station with an Achimedes spiral in concrete, making a honeycombed geodesic dome out of a sandwich of plastic sheets and soda cans, corrugated roofs out of concrete culverts, a pair of circular staircases modeled after an interlocking set in the Vatican, but painted yellow to stand out against the prairie's plainness. This list only scratches the surface. Robert Wilson's Fermilab is simply one of the unsung wonders of the age.

It's a wonder of the age all right but it's not unsung. The *World Book Encyclopedia* gave it a whole chapter in one of their annual supplements. It's called *Science Year, 1974.* Ask for it in your public library. I'll show excerpts here with their colored pictures reduced in size. The text is by the University of Wisconsin physics professor, Dr. Robert Marsh.

Robert Rathbun Wilson is director of the National Accelerator Laboratory (NAL), a vast $200-million installation of the Atomic Energy Commission (AEC), which sprawls across 6,800 acres of Illinois prairie 35 miles west of Chicago. The NAL was built to continue the search for new insights into the nature of matter by probing the internal workings of sub-nuclear particles. This laboratory is clearly the product of thousands of hands and minds, yet everywhere it bears two unmistakable Wilson imprints: One of Wilson the physicist, the other of Wilson the artist. For Robert Wilson is a most contradictory figure — a romantic individualist leading a great scientific team effort.

A map of the 4-mile, ringlike tunnel housing the NAL accelerator frames Wilson as he sits in his office. From here, his personal touch extends to every phase of the operation.

A visitor to the NAL site would have to look closely for clues of a major research laboratory. The heart of the project, a 4-mile ring of machinery designed to push protons up to 99.99 per cent of the speed of light, lies buried in a tunnel beneath untilled farmland. Were it not for one architecturally striking high-rise office building, strange and aloof in this rural setting, it would be easy to believe that the state of Illinois had taken over the land for a wildlife refuge.

The hundred or so farm buildings and low-cost houses that the NAL inherited when the site was purchased in 1967 still stand, although many were moved into a compact "village" that serves as the workplace for most of the laboratory's 1,000 employees. At the edge of the village stands a group of farmhouses. Their lonely dignity evokes the turn-of-the-century Midwestern mood of a Grant Wood

A sense of history led Wilson to combine old farmhouses for visitors' housing, and provide a haven for buffalo on the NAL fields.

painting. They provide housing for the hundreds of visiting scientists who come from throughout the world to use the NAL. The taste, the mood, and the practicality of the village are all pure Wilson.

"I couldn't bear the thought of just knocking them down," he explains, "especially the old farm buildings. Besides, this way we could move right in without waiting for construction." The fun of playing city planner in the layout of the village was one of the aspects of his job that Wilson likes to refer to as a "bonus". He had a hand in the design of nearly every building at NAL. He takes particular pride in the high-rise office building and in the 1,000-seat auditorium adjoining it. He also got the chance to apply his sculptor's talents to avoid a traditional eyesore. The metal towers that carry high-tension lines are his unique and attractive design.

In 1935, Wilson, a graduate student, went to work in the laboratory of Nobel prize-winning physicist Ernest O. Lawrence, who had just invented the cyclotron, a tiny ancestor of NAL's giant proton accelerator. While he completed his doctoral research on collisions between protons,

Wilson courted Jane Scheyer, an English literature major who came from San Francisco, across the bay from Berkeley. They were married in 1940, just before he left for his first job, at the new cyclotron laboratory at Princeton University, where he hoped to follow up his thesis research.

But fate had different plans in store for a nuclear physicist at that time. Wilson was one of a handful of specialists in this field on the East Coast, and his skills were commandeerred by Enrico Fermi. Fermi has just fled Fascist Italy and was working on uranium fission at Columbia University. The Princeton cyclotron was an essential tool in the informal "uranium project" launched by Fermi and other physicists before the federal government created the Manhattan Project. The Princeton group was assigned to study neutron capture in uranium.

In 1943, when J. Robert Oppenheimer opened the Los Alamos, N. Mex., laboratory where the first atomic bombs were designed and built, Wilson took his team there. He became the head of nuclear physics research though he was not yet 30 years old!

Los Alamos was a strange community, isolated from the world atop a desert mesa. Because the very existence of the laboratory was a secret, most of its staff members were rarely allowed to leave the site. Jane Wilson worked as a schoolteacher for the many children who were trapped there by their parent's work.

After the war, Wilson joined the scientists' fight to keep control of atomic energy out of military hands. Out of this political battle grew the Federation of American Scientists (FAS), a liberal organization often referred to as "the conscience of the physicists." Wilson served as the group's first chairman, and is still a member of the FAS advisory board.

Jane Wilson is an editor on the staff of "The Bulletin of the Atomic Scientists," a monthly journal on science and politics.

Returning to civilian research, Wilson spent the year 1946 designing a new cyclotron at Harvard University, and then accepted the post of director of nuclear studies at Cornell University in 1947. There he built a succession of increasingly powerful electron accelerators.

When the ABC wanted to build the super instrument for scientific study, there was an austerity mood in Washington. The original $300-million budget was cut to 250. Now Bob Wilson became a logical choice for builder. He had just completed an electron accelerator at Cornell University for 15 percent less than the original cost estimate. Although a much smaller machine, it was a cousin of the NAL giant. Using an excavating "mole", Wilson had built it under the beautiful Cornell campus without disturbing the surface.

To build the NAL machine on a stringent budget, Wilson cut out all margin of error that had been allowed in construction design. The tunnel holding the pipe in which the protons travel was originally designed as a massive, air-conditioned structure anchored in bedrock. It became a simple cut-and-fill concrete sewer pipe. The magnets were redesigned so they could be produced on an assembly line. They were to prove so inexpensive to build that Wilson found his budget would cover enough for a machine twice as big as the original Berkeley design. This meant that it could ultimately reach 400 GeV simply by drawing more electric power.

Even this economy drive felt the impact of Wilson the sculptor. He was delighted to find that his art-nouveau design for the stands on which the accelerator magnets rest would be cheaper to cast than a simple rectangular frame.

Of course, this approach was a gamble. In a device so complex, with every component designed to just barely do its job, something was bound to fail. Wilson hoped that correcting the inevitable failures would cost less than building in the safety factors. The risks were not his alone. Given the stringent economic mood in Washington, any serious mistake he made might spell the doom of particle physics research in America.

Wilson saved still more money by deliberately understaffing the lab. "People are happier and work better when they can see there's plenty to be done," he says. Just as at Cornell, chains of command were kept informal with Wilson intervening directly on all levels.

★   ★   ★   ★   ★

(These stars indicate fantastic technical problems encountered. I skip these in this condensation.)

The moment of triumph. Wilson led the NAL staff in a Chianti toast to celebrate the first successful acceleration of a proton beam to 200 GeV. This energy has since been doubled.

On March 1, 1972, the machine held a beam of protons in line for the 300,000 turns required to reach an energy of 200 GeV. A rising line on an oscilloscope screen told the tale. In minutes word spread around the lab. The control room became pandemonium as most of the scientists crowded in to savor the triumph. Bob Wilson led his staff in a toast with Italian Chianti wine, a tradition started among physicists when Fermi turned on the world's first nuclear reactor at the University of Chicago in December, 1942.

Wilson and his team had much to be proud of. Against many obstacles, the NAL staff had built a machine that was capable of reaching twice the proposed energy, four months ahead of the original target date. And when they finished, there was still money left in the budget. In an era when cost overruns, performance cutbacks, and production delays have become the rule in government projects, Wilson's triumph at NAL ranks as a minor miracle.

At the end of the day, Wilson the scientist heads for his studio in an old barn behind his house. There, he becomes Wilson the sculptor as he turns his hand to creating images in wood and stone.

Today Bob Wilson spends most of his time lecturing to other super scientists around the world. This summer (1984) he will be in China helping them build their first large accelerator in Beijing near the hallowed Ming Tombs.

I can't sign off without proclaiming a final facet in the brilliance of this man. The world acclaims his tangible art. I proclaim his linguistic art, his skill with the lilting phrase and the prose that approaches poetry. For examples consult his writings by way of the *Reader's Guide.* Or ask for the June 12, 1976 issue of *The New Republic.* The article that starts on page 21 is not by Bob. It's about Bob and his laboratory for adding to our sum of knowledge. It ends with his testimony before a Senate Investigating Committee where his words are lyric. He contends, in essence that the poet was right. Truth and beauty are synonymous. Keats found these in his *Grecian Urn.* Wilson finds them deep in the nucleus of his atom. Here's his testimony: Senator Pastore: *Is there anything in the hopes of this accelerator that involves the security of this country?* Dr. Wilson: *No sir, I do not believe so.* Senator Pastore: *Nothing at all?* Dr. Wilson: *It has to do with the respect with which we regard one another. It has to do with are we good painters, good sculptors, great poets. I mean all the things we really venerate and are patriotic about. It has nothing to do directly with defending our country except to make it worth defending.*

The latest book about Wilson is by Philip Hilts. It's called *Scientific Temperaments.* An up-coming one will be by Joe McGinniss who has written five best selling documentaries. He made his reputation when Nixon defeated Humphrey. That book detailed the process by which a politician could be packaged and sold like soup. Or cigarettes. His new book will be called *The Forbidden City* and tell the tale of our race with Hitler to produce the super weapon. During three frantic years all the great scientists in the free world — fifteen of them Nobel Prize winners — labored in isolated secrecy to design, build and test the first atomic bomb. I've talked with the still-youthful Joe and eulogized my famous cousin. In his book the talented writer will face the difficult task of evaluating the

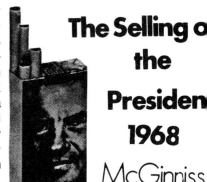

The Selling o
the
Presiden
1968
McGinniss

diverse personalities in that galaxy of genius confined on a desert. Consider just the leader alone, the beloved little "Oppy" who could speak six languages and whose genius rescued the world from the threat of Hitler. Yet he was later denounced by a Congressional Committee and denied security clearance. This because he had a brother who was a communist and he gave money to the party and refused to denounce all their doctrine. And that other controversial figure, Teller! The brilliant Hungarian developed the H bomb, defended Oppenheimer, then denounced Oppenheimer and wept when fellow scientists refused to shake his hand. He presents an enigma to any biographer.

I considered being one years ago. Horty and I had been in partial contact with our desert cousins via a secret P.O. Box in Las Vegas. And our son was part of that Manhattan Project. This was at Oak Ridge where the uranium piles were built and other projects carried on where huge power from the Tennessee Valley dams was required. Rog had finished his Officer's Training in the Navy and got the Manhattan job through his Todd School Physics teacher who was working there. But instead of writing my version of that isolated city at the frightening age of four-score, we retired to the tropics where I indulged a typewriter addiction by writing a family memoir and cooled a sea-fever by cruising the Caribbean and running a yacht-charter business in the Keys.

Sailing had been born into me and was eagerly adopted by a city-bred wife. My Nova Scotia father was the son of a ship builder. He went to sea as a boy in square riggers and started *his* son sailing in dingies at six. When the Japanese bombed Pearl Harbor, we turned Todd into a *Naval Academy.* It had long featured a sailing program but now that sport became a science and every graduate became a competent celestial navigator. Most entered Officers' Training but some, eager for action, became "Ninety Day Wonders," a program that turned out Warrant Officers. As soon as these could determine the angle of a heavenly body and add a few figures from an almanac they might find themselves in command of a vessel bound for a beach half a world away. Todd was a small school but in that vicious war we lost nearly 200 boys. Our son graduated in 1944. Seniors were regularly given a 10-day pre-commencement trip. Usually to Washington and the East in one of our sleeper buses. This class asked for a trip to Canada in our schooner. There's a page in our memoir headed **The Pact of Lake Michigan.** I'll reproduce it here:

Sea Hawk cockpit
June 6, 1944

D-Day. The night of the cross-channel invasion.

It is past midnight in the middle of that lake. Hortense and I are in our "captain's stateroom." This is aft. With skylight open we can hear the conversation in the cockpit. Young Rog is at the wheel. It is June 6. A fresh breeze is on our quarter and the schooner careens down the swell on a rumb line (198° True) between Grand Haven and Waukegan. The entire class stays on watch and the talk is of financing their planned future afloat, a round-the-world journey. It must be far in the future because a war is on and all are young and service-obligated. But Hitler's star has started down; Rommel is defeated in Africa; ANZAC troops are island-hopping the Pacific. Most of our group are signed for officer-training which will defer combat for awhile. They decide on a target date for their adventure: 1948. Each will sign a pact obligating him to contribute $250 a year for four years. This will go into a one-way pot with no refunds to any who back out. Optimism oozes. I hear Rog say: "I can persuade the Old Man to let us have *Sea Hawk.* He'll be a push-over if he's let in on part of the trip." At 0300 (that's nine in the morning in London) the radio (it's been giving us Guy Lombardo) crackels out: *Attention! This is the office of the Supreme Allied Command. General Eisenhower announces Normandy landings have been underway all night. One hundred and fifty thousand men in LST's and supporting vessels have crossed the channel in heavy weather. They have breached most of the enemy's defenses. Air cover has been complete. Only at Caen has a Panzer division turned our forces back. The long awaited D-Day has come.* That was at three o'clock our time. Further bulletins continued. Sleep was out of the question. We changed course; went into Racine for breakfast and a day of happy slumber at a coal dock.

After graduation, the class told me what my cockpit eavesdropping had earlier taught me, the details of their grandiose plan. Thousands of dollars had been subscribed; none collected. It would start accumulating soon, they said, and once in hand would cover all expenses of outfitting and living. All they needed was a ship. Could they use *Sea Hawk* for maybe two years and would I join them for part of the time? I concealed my envy, hid my supercilious smile, lied, and said "I think we can work something out." I had no faith but great empathy. I, too, had dreamed that improbable round-the-world dream.

But these kids meant it. At the end of a year they had two grand in the bank. I was forced to take them seriously. I was also forced to disillusion them about their dear love, *Sea Hawk*. A survey had discovered that the ship, once owned by FDR and berthed at his summer home on Campobello Island, was approaching her end. The backbone, from stem to horn-timber was soft. Still safe for the Great Lakes where a day's sail could reach a port but unfit for crossing oceans.

Search for a replacement covered both coasts. They found *Yankee Girl* in Stonington, the 17th century harbor on upper Long Island Sound near Mystic. They didn't make their target date of 1948 but later, with two brides aboard, they had their long planned voyage.

Here's Emily and young Rog on their tropic honeymoon. I've been quoting from our family memoir published when we turned eighty, that biblical cut-off time for any life abundant. The psalmist, you'll remember, tells us: *The days of our years are three-score and ten.*

If, by reason of strength, they be four-score, yet is that strength labour and sorrow and soon cut off. But the Hills beat the odds. Horty had seven more years of glorious life working for Peace. We're putting out a new edition of that memoir as her memorial. It will have much new material and include excerpts from other books her children have now written.

One Man's
time and chance.

A Memoir of Eighty Years 1895/1975

ROGER HILL

Childhood

Memorial Edition

Hortense Gettys Hill

Parenthood

Grandparenthood

Great-Grandparenthood

Sunset

This is a reduced facsimile of the 8½ × 11 colored cover with its memorial inscription.

On page 7 I said that Todd's involvement with the Quakers sent the Hills to Hiroshima. Here's the way it happened: In 1946 America had a growing feeling of guilt over the suffering of survivors. This led to the forming in 1947 of our *Atomic Bomb Casualty Commission* which sent scientists to Hiroshima to study A-bomb diseases. An anthropologist from Antioch college, Dr. Earle Reynolds, was chosen to head the work on radiation damage. Antioch and Todd had co-operated for years. When Earle and his wife, Barbara, decided to leave their son, Tim, in America until they could establish a Japanese home, they brought the boy to us. On a wall, Earle saw pictures of our schooners and the conversation shifted at once from the boy's curriculum to the father's addiction to the sea and to sailing. This was a surprising fact. The scientist who labored in a laboratory had never lived near an ocean. But he had read the Joshua Slocum classic, *Sailing Alone Around the World* and never lost a desire to duplicate that feat. I told him the desire now seemed to be a possibility. He was headed for a seaport which would surely have a shipyard and probably have cheap labor. When asked for suggestions on size and type, I shamelessly pontificated: "At least forty feet if you want to stay off-shore in comfort and not more then fifty if it's to be family-sailed. A double-ender for sure and an outboard rudder. Probably a ketch rig or maybe a staysail schooner. Four years later he and his family sailed out of Hiroshima on the ketch, *Phoenix.* They circled the globe and wrote a book which is one of the best sea tales ever. It's in almost every public library. Ask for it. I'll show a reduced picture of its jacket.

Earle also wrote a second book entitled *The Forbidden Journey.* This is an account of his arrest and trial when the family, as a protest, sailed into the testing zone for the hydrogen bomb. Our AEC (Atomic Energy Commission) had proclaimed the Marshall Islands and a great area of the ocean (400,000 square miles) closed to all shipping. This was an affront to the centuries-old *Freedom of the Seas* tradition and the international law upholding this. Protests were made but, except for the Soviets, these were mostly token ones. When Phoenix crossed the boundary, a U.S. Coast Guard cutter pulled along side and proclaimed them under arrest. They were escorted to our Naval Base at Kwajalein where the yacht was impounded and the adults flown to Honolulu. Earle was tried and sentenced to six months in jail. American opinion, however, was solidly in his favor and he spent little time behind bars. In a later trial he was acquitted.

Papers on the mainland were full of another story in those days. This was the bringing of *Phoenix* to Honolulu. Word had come from the boys in "Kwaj" that the yacht was in danger of sinking because worms had eaten throught the planking. Earle asked the court for permission to bring his boat to Hawaii for repairs. This was denied and with reluctance he agreed to let Barbara do it. With only 2 boys for a crew! Just Ted and his Japanese friend, Nick Mikami! The Navy tried to dissuade them. It proclaimed the trip without an adequate crew, foolhardy. Barbara sailed on August 13th, 1958. Based on her ship's average run, she could be expected in 30 days. When 40 passed, her "missing ship" became a news story. When 50 passed, there were daily bulletins; reports of a "violent storm" a few days after her departure. Then tales of fishing boats picking up flotsam which they identified as from *Phoenix*. On the 60th day, the yacht sailed serenely into Honolulu and made headlines across America. Their radio had failed ; their motor had failed; their wind had failed. But not their Skipper. That December, she received nominations for Time Magazine's "Man of the Year!"

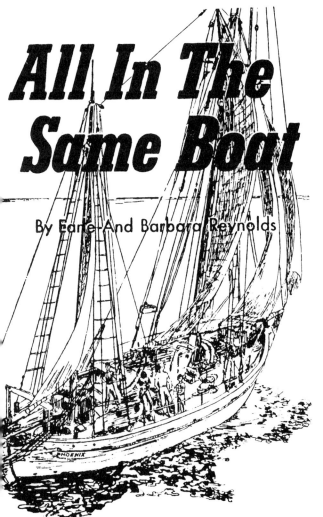

All In The Same Boat

By Earle And Barbara Reynolds

ALL IN THE SAME BOAT

An American Family's Adventures on a Voyage Around The World

by Earle and Barbara Reynolds

THIS IS the chronicle of a family that made a dream come true. Ten years ago, Earle Reynolds, a U.S. anthropologist studying bomb casualties at Hiroshima, decided the time had come to realize the desire he'd had ever since reading Slocum's journal, to build his own boat and sail around the world. Without knowing seamanship or marine architecture—or much Japanese—he managed to get the *Phoenix* constructed near Hiroshima and shortly after set out with his wife, little girl, young son, a cat and three Japanese who'd never been on the high seas before. The voyage lasted 5 years, 9 months, 26 days; they visited 122 ports, spent 649 days at sea, sailed 54,359 sea miles (about 62,520 land miles).

The book is full of yarns and intimate details of how they worked it out, from educating daughter Jessica, to getting on in a 50-foot ketch with two sexes, two languages and

(*Continued on back flap*)

25

The Todd School Closes!!

Here's another picture from that family memoir. It was taken in 1950 and we're shown aboard *Sea Hawk* in Lake Michigan. We would close the Todd School soon. This because it was an anomaly that could have been carried on only by something akin to the Ford Foundation. It had half as many faculty members as students! They had been with us since the Depth of the Great Depression when public school teachers were being paid with "script". Ours were being paid with little cash but large amenities including joy in their jobs. All were now ready to retire including Horty. She spent a year on *Yankee Girl* with the honeymoon couples while I opened up a yacht charter business in the tropics. This left our summers free for world travel.

This from the memoir
written 10 years ago

Sea Hawk
1950

This is your grandmother, young at 55, who met the adventure of sailing (as she now meets the adventure of dying) with fortitude and with humor, qualities nurtured out there by the wind and the rain and the stars and the sea.

Todd catalogues were written and printed by boys. This cover was drawn by Orson Welles when he was 14. It is his conception of the main campus. From the stable and riding ring in the upper right-hand corner, a private road led to our farm and airport.

TODD
A COMMUNITY DEVOTED TO
BOYS
AND THEIR
INTERESTS

Now back to Barbara. This gallant lady is much more than an intrepid sailor. She is the nearest thing to a saint that our family has ever known. Her life has been one long dedication to the poor and the oppressed. She was the first head of the *World Friendship Center* in Hiroshima. The love and devotion of the survivors there (the *hibakusca*) is total and touching. On a visit to that city, she arranged for us to spend days in such a home. The family consisted of a father, mother and two surviving children. Before the bomb there had been six. They had one room for cooking, dining, sleeping and praying. This at a shrine in the corner. We ate at a table slightly above floor level with our

Barbara at the trial in Honolulu

feet in a sunken area that could be heated. We slept on tatami mats that were reasonably soft but the oval "pillows" made of wood had to be discarded in favor of folded clothing. Bathing was in a communal bathhouse where we showered, rinsed, and then inched our way down into steaming water. The trick is to not agitate it. This makes it unbearable. Our departure was touching. The formal bows on arrival now became embraces! These for Americans who had killed their children and left them suffering with leukemia and cancer. Their forgiveness was not a tribute to us but rather to our friend, Barbara-san. That suffix is one of endearment.

I've used the word, *Saint.* Do I exaggerate? Listen and then judge for yourself. She has used every dollar of an inheritance and every ounce of her strength on the unfortunate of this world. She helped Wilmington College, the Quaker school in Ohio, establish their Peace Resource Center with its library of bomb-related books, slides and tapes. 500 of their volumes are in Japanese. Some of these are her translations. She used her last cent taking a *Hiroshima-Nagasaki Peace Pilgrimage* around the world. Now in her seventies and in her widowhood, she lives in Long Beach, California, with a Vietnamese family she has adopted. She works on a minimum salary for the Cambodian Relief Committee.

Sainthood? Yes. I canonize her by an authority higher than any Pope. In the *Sermon on the Mount* a questioner asks *Lord, when saw I thee hungered and fed thee? When saw I thee naked and clothed thee? Or a stranger and I took thee in?* Christ's answer: *Inasmuch as ye have done it unto one of the least of these, my brethren, ye have done it unto me.*

Postscript: Barbara's widowhood is the grass variety. Earle is now married to a Japanese girl! I judge not that I be not judged. The ever-forgiving Barbara does the same.

When Harry Truman Dropped that Bomb!
Was he wise or was he wanton?

The man from Missouri became President just at the time America became master of the world. This mastery was assured that night of September 16 when the first atomic bomb lit up the desert at Alamagordo. Should we have demonstrated our dominance by having the *Enola Gay* drop its load in a living forest and kill 100,000 trees instead of in a living city and kill 100,000 humans? We wonder. One thing, at least, is sure: We lost the **moral highground** we might have taken in our race with Russia. Later, we did assume some **highground** with our **Marshall Plan** and it paid great dividends. It rebuilt Europe and deterred, for a while, Soviet expansionism.

If some of us wondered about the Truman decision, few others did. There was dancing in the streets. Joy was unconfined. **Hooray! That makes two World Wars where we've shown 'em. Now let's get back to Normalcy.** But "Normalcy" was gone forever.

Hortense was one of the worriers. Her grandson, Todd Tarbox, has a letter from her that reads: "I was living alone on Sea Hawk that week and grieving over the death of Jim White (a classmate of our son who had just been killed in the war) and when I heard the Hiroshima news I thought the world had come to its end. I got in the dinghy and rushed to the cottage. Joanne greeted me with *'Now no one in the world is safe.'* How true, how true."

Viewing History with Hindsight

Truman defended his sacrifice of Japanese civilians claiming it saved the lives of a far greater number of American soldiers. It was a reasonable assumption considering the *kamikaze* tactics at the time. He was wrong because we know now that Emperor Hirohito had, the day after Nagasaki, decided on surrender. He wrote to his high command "We must now endure the unendurable and suffer the insufferable." Also it saved Japan from invasion by Russia whose islands practically touch Japan at *La Perious Strait*. Without our show of strength plus chutzpah, Stalin would have marched into much of Japan as he marched into much of Eastern Europe right after the Postdam Conference. A Japanese foreign correspondent, *Kenzo Suziki,* has written: "We are glad the Russians did not come in and occupy us. Despite the horrors and the suffering caused by the bomb, we recognize the influence of Hiroshima in this fact."

"Truman was the last citizen President Since then; only Emperors"

That's a line from Robert Ferrell's new biography (Viking Press) of the wonderful little man who had great assurance but no pretense. Here's an anecdote: The Hills sailed into Key West one night and docked in the yacht harbor facing Roosevelt Boulevard. I woke up at dawn. Making coffee in the galley might wake a wife so I decided on a hamburger stand across the street. One customer sat on a stool with his back to me. He wore a cheap jacket, fantastically flowered. I sat down beside him assuming he was a tourist. His cheerful "Good Morning" was a shock. I stuttered out a "Good Morning Mr. President." He made some small talk about fishing conditions and the weather. Then he excused himself and went striding off down the street. Were Secret Service men around? Probably. But I looked carefully and could see none. It was well known that Truman used our submarine base in Key West as a winter White House and that he took morning walks. But *this* much informality! It was amazing then. It would be unthinkable now.

Epilouge

Once more a Peace Movement is alive in our land. And in Europe. And even in the Soviet Union. Yes, it's stifled and hard to see in Moscow but in Gorki and on the Volga we've found friendliness, curiosity and envy. Rulers of Russia are still as ruthless as the Romanoffs but their poliburo grows potbellied and their poeple grow restless. Their grandparents were illiterate serfs. Today they can read and write. *The Voice of America* is forbidden but this fact whets their appetite and a hidden one was shown to us. Time is on our side.

With the Soviets, yes. But with the terrorists, no. Time is on *their* side and the whole world may soon be held hostage by a few desperate or demented men. The nuclear genie is out of the bottle and can never be put back. Scientists tell us that today a small device exploded in the parking lot of a nuclear plant could crack it open and release the destructive power of a ten ton megaton bomb or the equivalent of ten million tons of TNT! No solution is in sight for our dreadful dilemma but surely sane men and women should now unite to find one. Instead, we remain adversaries of the Soviets and act like two children continuing a quarrel inside a building that is burning.

The Script of

Rip Van Winkle
RENASCENT

An Allegory for an Atomic Age

Cast of Characters

Most theater programs list the "credits" of a cast, their previous accomplishments. This play was produced 47 years ago. The prep-school boys who were the leads and the 7th graders who were the little gremlins ("mugging" to Dutch dialect voices) are now in their 50's. Their credits are many but all *after* the fact of any show business. *Rip* was played by Gahan Wilson, now a famous cartoonist. *Derrick Van Bummel* was played by Jon Geis, now a famous Manhattan psychologist. The *Waiter* and chief comic was Bill Fields who stayed in the music business through many successes. Then he shifted to law and became a noted tax expert. The philosophers and sages, Rick Avery, Dan Donnellan, Chuck Mattes and Mark Nerem are top business men. As are the gremlins: Chess Will, Tommy Corbett, Dave Anderson, Jimmy Harris, Sandy Gardener and Chris Welles. This last was a girl, Orson's daughter, now a writer of Scott, Foresman text books.

Authors

These were faculty members: Roger Hill, Pat Armstrong, Sandy Smith and Hascy Tarbox who also designed the sets and costumes, drew the cartoons and pretty much ran the show. Carl Hendrickson, Todd's Music Director, furnished the tunes. Orson Welles was busy on *Citizen Kane* at the time but made 2 trips to our set to see his daughter and give us ideas for all those special-effects.

Later, he toned down my certitude about a quick solution to our global dilema. I wrote the optimistic ending while men and women of good will from all over the world were sitting in the San Francisco Conference drafting a United Nations charter. We knew that Wilson's League had failed but this was a new world. War was now suicide and Tennyson's vision our **only** solution. Alas, we're not ready for it but there's no other way out. A Federation of the World must come. It's either that or extinction. At least we're still alive so there's still hope. And work to be done.

As the picture starts, the camera discovers a dwarf walking toward us on a rocky ledge. He holds a scroll and as he unrolls the parchment, the camera moves in to read:

**To our Respected and Munificent
Patron, The Audience:**

**We bring you a Tale of Fantasy,
an Allegory, Frankly Fabulous
Albeit Firmly Factual.**

**This is a Modern Version of that old
Morality Play, "Everyman."**

**It was Written, Set to Music, Acted,
Photographed, and Sound Recorded
by members of
THE TODD SCHOOL
on their campus at
WOODSTOCK, ILLINOIS
It is entitled
RIP VAN WINKLE, RENASCENT**

*Derrick Van Bummel, Washington Irving's Schoolmaster,
will now take you under his competent care.*

*(The picture dissolves into the exterior of a village school. Then the camera moves inside to discover, at his schoolmaster's desk, **Derrick Van Bummel**. He senses the presence of visitors and turns)*

Van B:

Good evening. To begin, let me tell you something of our village and our people in the year of our Lord, 1774. Whoever has made a voyage up the Hudson must remember the Catskill Mountains. *(He goes to his wall map.)* At the foot of these mountains lies our village *(the map dissolves into a view of the village)* a few miles up the river from the thriving city of New York *(we dissolve again to a harbour view of the small colonial city)* which has mushroomed so amazingly in its one hundred years of post-Stuyvesant rule under the British. In our Village lives a kind but sadly bewildered and confused man named Rip Van Winkle. *(Bummel walks toward the door. The camera picks up a divided Dutch doorway. The upper half swings open and **Rip Van Winkle** appears.)*

Rip:

Hello Derrick. Still tending school?

Van B:

I was about to close up for the day, Rip. And you?

Rip:

Going down to the village. I've lost Wolf. He chased a rabbit out of sight and never did come back. Coming along? *(Rip waves a farewell to his friend and disappears. The schoolmaster leans out over the lower door and calls down the street to him)*

Van B:

I <u>am</u> sort of holding school at the moment. *(He turns and speaks to the camera)* That, as you are aware, unless you're wearing a dunce cap in the corner, is America's best known escapist, Rip Van Winkle. Mr. Irving has seen to it that his wife is usually to be found in close pursuit. And such is the case even now.

Voice:

Rip! Rip Van Winkle.

Van B:

Dame Van Winkle. A major factor in Rip's general bewilderment. I'm going down to the village now and I hope you'll care to come along. *(he reaches for his hat on a wall peg)* In front of our local pub we are quite apt to find an extremely vocal group of philosophers and sages. *(He leaves and the scene dissolves to an inn yard. Four pompous Dutch burghers are drinking at a table. They go into a song).*

OPENING CHORUS

The Four:	We're philosophers. We're sages, With the opening song required on all stages. We're the Katskill Walter Lipmanns here in session Thinking deep and drinking deep for you.
First:	Nothing can disturb our peace and quiet, Bow and arrow, musket shot or riot.
The Four:	We're philosophers. We're sages. We'll write columns for the press in future ages.
First:	I'm an eggspert on finance und costs und vages.
Second:	I shall specialize on International phases.
Third:	I'm zuper brain dot bursts all vorldy cages.
The Waiter:	I'll write what they'll really read—the comic pages.
First:	I'm Van Hoozen
Second:	Van Boozen
Third:	Van Schnoozen
Fourth:	Van Burp.
The Waiter:	I'm Schultz.

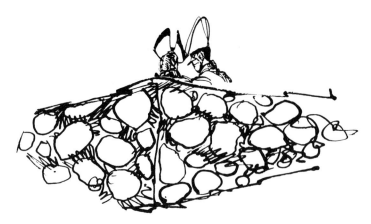

During a music vamp, **Rip** *and* **Van Bummel** *enter the inn yard.*
Rip *points to the group and sings to his friend.)*

Rip:
> **They'll talk of death and what's as sure, they'll talk of taxes**
> **While the world spins merrily upon its axis.**

First: **The peasants have to work from morn till sundown.**

Second: **We're the ones who'll see they damn well do.**

First: **Let the hewers of wood carry water.**

Second: **We'll show them it's their duty and they oughter.**

The Four: **We're philosophers. We're sages.**
> **We'll write columns for the press in future ages.**

First: **I'm Van Hoozen.**

Second: **Van Boozen.**

Third: **Van Schnoozen.**

Fourth: **Van Burp.**

The Four: *(Before the Waiter can get in his line)* **He's Schultz.**
(After the song the camera turns to **Rip** *and* **Van Bummel** *who are by the garden wall.* **Rip** *looks past his friend and says)*

Rip:
> **Oh, Oh! Here comes more advice—My wife!** *(He quickly hides)* **Shh—I went home.** *(Dame Winkle, still hot on* **Rip's** *trail, enters the scene.)*

Dame: **Did you see that loafer?**

Van B: **He was here a little while ago. He told me he was going home.**

Dame: **He'd better. The new preacher, Van Goodykuntz, is coming to supper. He promised me he'd give him a good talk.** *(She hurries off.* **Rip** *comes out of hiding.)*

Rip:

I can't take it, Derrick. I'm off to the mountains.

Van B:

Oh Rip, not again! That's a never-never land. Life has to be faced, Rip. And improved.

Rip:

Let the wind bags do the improving. It's an occupational disease.

Van B:

No Rip, you're wrong. The improving is up to you and me. To the little guys. These colonies can be turned into a great land for our children. But it won't be done by King George. It won't even be done by Ben Franklin. It's got to be done by you and me.

Rip:

All right, Derrick. I won't go up in the mountains. At least not far. But I can't go home tonight.

Van B: Rip.

Rip: Yes.

Van B: Promise me one thing.

Rip: Sure.

Van B: No grog.

Rip: *(after a sigh)* No grog.

(Rip starts off as the scene fades out. The fade-in discloses a series of mountain-climbing shots. As Rip gains altitude, the colors gain brilliancy.The nature of the scenery loses reality. Background music has picked up the tune, "Muddled Life" and now a Dwarf with a concertina peeks from behind a rock. Here is the source of the music we have heard. Rip continues to climb. Another furtive Dwarf is seen playing the tune on a fiddle. Rip is very weary as he struggles to the top of a final pinnacle. More Dwarfs with instruments are up there to meet

*him but they duck behind rocks unseen. **Rip** is very dejected as he sings:)*

MUDDLED LIFE

Oh I lead a muddled, huddled life,
My only aim is to avoid all strife.
If King George wants his tax
It can't hurt Catskill Dutch
And federation won't improve us much.
Let Patrick Henry say he'll choose to die
For the other colonies no thanks, not I.
To be left alone is all I beg,
My life is like a scrambled egg,
Just an I-don't-knowish, status-quoish guy.

*(As the song ends a **Dwarf** peeks from behind a rock and calls:)*

Dwarf 1:

> **Rip Van Winkle.** *(**Rip** hears it. He looks in the wrong direction, then back at the camera. Another **Dwarf** peeks from the other side and calls)*

Dwarf 2:

> **Rip Van Winkle.** *(Again **Rip** looks the wrong way. Then in the right direction. He does a double-take and in astonishment cries)*

Rip:

> **Hey! Who are you?** *(No answer. Some other **Dwarfs** are now creeping in behind **Rip**.)* **I said, who are you? Speak up you little runt.** *(The first **Dwarf** now has a club behind **Rip** and raises it slowly preparatory to beaning him.)*

Dwarf 2:

Easy Hans. Dot vouldn't be necessary. He iss de type vould react easy mit persuasion. *(He pours a drink while* **Rip** *turns, frightened, sees another* **Dwarf** *behind him.)*

Rip:

Er..Who..Who are you?

Dwarf 2:

You mean right now? *(He is handing* **Rip** *a drink.)*

Rip:

Well..uh..I mean whenever you have time to answer.

Dwarf 2:

Nein. Mine meaning iss, iss your meaning who are ve right now or who iss it ve effer vere yet?

Rip:

Well..er..I'm sorry. I'm a little confused. Who are you right now?

Dwarf 2:

Led's see. Sometimes it iss confused I get it also. Vot time iss it?

Dwarf 3:

Yeh, what time is it?

Dwarf 4:

It's...It's the reign of Louie the 15th. That reminds me, Louis should be back with us soon.

Dwarf 5:

The time? It's about a quarter to the age of steam.

Dwarf 8:

(He takes out a pocket astrolobe) It's eggsactly seventeen hundert und sigsty-nine. So...Who am I yet? Right now I represent my compatriots in de matter of de brew. Prosit. *(He fills a mug and hands it to* **Rip.)*

Rip:

I know. I've heard of you. You're Hendrick Hudson's men. From the Half Moon.

De villagers, dey say so. Goot.

Dwarf 1:

De fact is, we're de...(bashful) ah, should I tell 'im, men?

Dwarf 4:

Sure. He's just a little guy.

Dwarf 1:

Ah, I don't want you to tink we're boastin' none but we're de..we're de heels of history.

Dwarf 4:

Yeah. Past and present.

Rip:

I don't get it. But I don't like it either. (He gets up and calls) Oh, Derrick!

Dwarf 4:

Who's Derrick?

Dwarf 2:

Van Bummel from de American colonies. Another little guy. (To Rip) Van Bummel's a long vey off now Van Winkle und ve're your friends. Play along vid us and ve'll bring you sweet dreams and teach you how to bowl.

Rip:

But what are you doing here?

Dwarf 2:

Vell...dis iss a sort of a hide out.

Rip:

Hide out?

Dwarf 1:

Yeah. We're de gremlins.

Rip:

Gremilins?

Dwarf 1:

Yeah—Big gremlins—Outa history books.

Rip:

Wait a minute. You say this is a hide out. What do you mean?

Dwarf 2:

Did you effer hear of Valhalla yet?

Er...Yes.

Dwarf 2:

Vell—Valhalla dis isn't. For de vorld's heros sort of Valhalla iss. Ve're more....how did Hans say?...history's heels yet.

Dwarf 1:

Yeah. Vacationing between jobs.

Dwarf 2:

Und diss place has eferyting got. Eggvitable climite. Baths from hot springs. Regreation.

Dwarf 1:

Yeah...good bowlin'. Fresh tunderbolts.

Dwarf 2:

Unt most imbortant, a view of eferyting happening in de entire vorld yet. Look. *(He leads Rip to the edge of cliff and they look over) New York—London—Asia.*

Rip:

Say! I'm beginning to believe you boys. Are you really big shots out of history books?

Dwarf 1:

Yeah, dat's us. De tough guys.

Dwarf 6:

Oh not all tough. I've been quite refined in many of my incarnations.

Dwarf 1:

Okeh. Okeh. Okeh. He's da refined type. Machiavelli, he was.

Dwarf 6:

Fact is I've just returned from a most interesting assignment.

Dwarf 4:

Fritz vas British dis time. But he vorked on de liddle guys..in Bengal. Show him Fritz.

Dwarf 6:

(He changes his pansy diction for a British accent) **Oh by all means. Raw-ther Pip Pip.** *(He is instantly changed into costume and make-up of a British officer)* **Clive of India, old thing. Black hole of Calcutta you know.**

Rip:

I must be getting pretty drunk. I'd swear he just turned into a red coat. I don't get it.

Dwarf 1:

Brudder, what have we been tellin ya? Name any of de heels. Dat's us. Name a tough one—any tough one. Dat's me.

Rip:

A tough one? King George?

Dwarf 1:

A tough one I say....A really, really *tough* one.

Rip:

Er...Attila?

Dwarf 1:

Attila, he says. Now dere's one was me. Perfessor, would you oblige for de little guy. *(The Dwarf with the concertina obliges with an introductory glissade. As Dwarf 1 starts the song, THAT WAS ME, he changes, before Rip's astonished eyes into the character of Atilla)*

THAT WAS ME SONG

Atilla called the Hun
he made the Romans run.
He made his mark with methods stark
He didn't need no gun
But even on Atilla
Horns looked silla.
That was me.

*(As the Atilla song ends, the camera pans to **Dwarf 2** and we see his body dissolve into that of **Ghengis Kahn** singing his song to a mystified and drunken **Rip**.)*

GHENGIS KAHN SONG

Dwarf 2:
You've heard of Ghengis Khan
Whose hordes came down upon
The poor plebian, European
Folks so pale and wan.
We'll shake the hand that is the hand
For Ghengis Khan was me.

*(**Rip**, completely confused, staggers across the set as he sings:)*

RIP'S DRUNK SONG

We're...all...
Drinking to much grog.
Let's go home and call the thing a day.
My...legs...
Feel like a pollywog
Please...go...away.

*(The **Dwarf** with the concertina sings:)*

YOU CAN'T LEAVE US NOW

You can't leave us now
We've got you in our power
You'll start to drool
And surely you'll
Be sleeping in an hour
Stick around, you'll love it
Rip Van Winkle stay with me.

(During the song other **Dwarfs** *have led* **Rip** *to a bed on a rocky ledge. When he lies down, a vision of* **Van Bummel's** *face appears above him and talk-sings these lines:)*

> **Rip, where have you gone?**
> **Remember if you're wise**
> **Those evil men up in the glen**
> **Are against the little guys.**
> **Don't let them use their wily ways.**
> **Van Winkle, stay with me.**

*(***Rip*** *tries to rise, staggers, and continues with his drunken song.)*

> **I must be getting home,**
> **My mind is in a fog.**
> **I promised Derrick Bummel**
> **That I wouldn't hit the grog.**

(The dwarfs surround **Rip**, *leading him back to his bed as one of them sings:)*

> **Van Bummel's awfully far away.**
> **Just follow, follow us.**

(The music modulates into the **Dwarf's***)*

SLUMBER SONG
> **Go to sleep. Close your eyes.**
> **Let that silly fool, Van Bummel**
> **Plan his bright new day.**
> **Go to sleep. No more sighs.**
> **Lulla, Lullaby**

(The **Dwarfs** *tiptoe off and the scene fades out. It fades in on the New York city skyline and the Yankee Doodle motif which opened the play. Transparent* **Ghost of Van Bummel** *walks across the scene dressed in the uniform of the Continental army. When he notices the audience, he turns, stops, and speaks to us.)*

Van B:

Hello there. Remember me? Van Bummel, the schoolmaster. I died back there somewhere you know. The villagers saw me off with the Continental Army at the beginning of the war.

Voice:

Wait a minute. Who did you say you are?

Van B:

I am what I always was, Derick Van Bummel. Only in life is there change.

Voice:

Where did you die?

Van B:

The exact spot is immaterial. The villagers said that I died by the bridge at Concord. I'll say that I died again in the muck of a trench on Bunker Hill. Again on that third morning at Gettysburg. Again at Chateau Thierry, at Argonne.

Voice:

Then you're a perpetual warrior?

Van B:

No, thank God. At least not yet. If Rip can be awakened I'll avoid that fate.

Voice:

Has Rip, the little guy, slept all this time? Why, it's 1920.

Van B:

Well, yes, he's slept much of the time. Though our wars have usually roused him. In fact, to amazing feats of coordinated effort. Some of our depressions have stirred him too. Possibly he can be roused even now. If you'll excuse me. I'm on my way to make that attempt.

*(During the above conversation, the background has shifted to a battle ground with a dead soldier hanging in the barbed wire. Now it dissolves again, this time into our mountain trail. **Van Bummel** is climbing it)*

Voice:

No, I don't get it. Who did you say you are?

45

Van B:

A simple man but one privileged in death to see beyond the years. I was at Philadelphia when they signed the constitution. I crossed the western plains in a thousand covered wagons. I stood with Lincoln on the platform at Gettysburg. I was with Wilson at Versailles.

Voice:

All right, let's put it this way. What are you?

Van B:

Now I hear I'm Uncle Sam. I'm Mr. Wiskers. The old guy with the striped pants in your morning newspaper cartoon. *(He has reached the top and he calls out in front of him)* Halloooo, Rip Van Winkle, Rip. Can you hear me? *(We cut to **Rip,** just stirring from sleep on his couch. **Van Bummel** enters.)*

Rip: Oh? You? What's up this time?

Van B:

Rip, you can't relax again. You stayed awake to win the great war. While you sleep we're losing the peace. Come here!

*(The camera is zooming down to the American continent and finally to the Main Street of a small city. A model T Ford is pulling up to an elaborate home. A flapper gets out of the car. **Van Bummel** shouts:)*

LOOK ON AMERICA!
SEE WHAT YOU'VE DONE
IN THE YEAR OF OUR LORD
THE UKULELE AND THE FORD
NINETEEN TWENTY ONE!

FLAPPERS!
SHORT SKIRTS!
HAIR CUT BOB!
PROHIBITION!
RULE BY MOB!

(A gunman in a dark alley shoots a cop.)

RIOTS! RED SCARES!
KLANSMEN MARCHING!

(We see a burning cross on a hilltop)

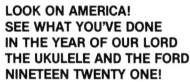

(A newsboy holds up his paper and calls headlines.)

> **ELECTION LANDSLIDE!**
> **WARREN G. HARDING!**

*(**Van Bummel** shouts out scandals of the 20's while we see a reader turn to a page for each one.)*

> **BIG BILL THOMPSON!**
> **AL CAPONE!**
> **SECRETARY FALL!**
> **TEAPOT DOME!**

(Now we see the newsboy call more headlines:)

> **BIG BULL MARKETS!**
> **FOUR DOLLAR WHEAT!**

(An indifferent citizen buys a paper, reads about the inflation and then comments:)

> **EUROPE HASN'T**
> **ENOUGH TO EAT.**

*(The Recession sets in and **Van Bummel** shouts:)*

> **NOW THE MARKET**
> **TUMBLES!**

(The newsboy holds up his paper and calls out:)

> **WHEAT'S A BUCK!**

(The same indifferent citizen reads this news and comments:)

> **IT'S ONLY THE FARMERS**
> **WHO'RE OUTA LUCK.**

*(We see **Rip** down there in modern clothes looking into a grocery window. He feels for money in his pocket, finds some, and enters the store. **Van Bummel** continues his comment:*

> **HERE'S A LITTLE GUY,**
> **THE COMMON MAN**
> **GETTING ALONG**
> **AS BEST HE CAN.**
> **HIS JOBS ARE FEWER**
> **THINGS ARE TOUGH**
> **BUT HE CAN STILL**
> **SCRAPE UP ENOUGH.**

(Now we see four coon-skin-coated collegians doing a college yell:)

THE COUNTRY'S GONE COLLEGIATE!
MONEY COMES FROM PA!
FOOTBALL! HIP FLASKS!
RAH! RAH! RAH!

*(Again, **Van Bummel** answers:)*

BUT THE LITTLE GUY ISN'T IN THAT GAME.
HE'S OUTA WORK SINCE DEPRESSION CAME.

*(Again we see **Rip** standing in front of that grocery. This time when he feels in his pocket for money he finds none and turns away to pick up a butt from the sidewalk.)*

EVEN BUTTS ARE FEW. HE LIVES ON STEW.

*(We see **Rip** standing in a breadline. Then the camera takes us back to the mountaintip where **Bummel** points to **Rip** and shouts:)*

IN 1921—THAT'S YOU!

(Note: This is the almost forgotten "Recession" of 1921. It was quickly over and was followed by the "Boom" years of the later 1920's. The "Great Depression" began with Hoover's stock market crash of October, 1929.)

Rip:
Derrick, I'll stay awake now. I promise.

Van B:
If I could only beleive that, Rip. *(we hear the music of the Dwarfs)*

Rip:
Listen! It's my friends, the little men.

Van B:
Your friends!

Rip:
I wonder what shapes they'll be in this time.

Van B:
Whatever shapes they're in, they're never your friends.

Rip:
You'd better stay with me then.

Van B:

I'm powerless, Rip. I can only fight them through you. My immortality, in fact my very existence vanishes when they appear. *(Van Bummel is gradually fading out of the scene)* Please, Rip. Stand up to them.

Rip:

Wait, Derrick. I need your help. *(He is vanished)* Derrick!

*(The vamp of another song starts. During it, our **Dwarfs**, now dressed as **International Diplomats** appear marching across the elaborate courtyard of an embassy. On one side a hanging sign shows a lion, rampant, and the words, LOWER MORONICA. During the first verse the diplomats enter another scene labeled UTTER DELUSIA and finally they exit and reappear climbing **Rip's** mountain trail, carrying bombs, and singing their*

SONG OF THE DIPLOMATS

> *We are diplomatic boys and we love a lot of noise*
> *But you mustn't think we mean to do you harm.*
> *Though we deal in bombs and treaties*
> *We devour bowls of wheaties*
> *And that's the major reason for our charm.*
> *Though we often times have friction*
> *We've a common predilection*
> *And on one thing we are all of us agreed,*
> *It's our solemn, bounded duty*
> *To steal any kind of booty*
> *Such as oil or any bases that we need.*

(Now they go into a dance with the bombs they carry. These are the old fashion kind, basketball size, with sputtering fuses. As they dance, the Diplomats continue their song:)

You no doubt are all agog—in a sort of mental fog
As to why we carry these about with us.
They're the symbols of our trade,
Knowing that they may be sprayed
The other side is not so apt to fuss.

*(Their song is over but their dance continues to a climax when one **Diplomat** rolls his bomb up the ravine. At the top it explodes into a huge cloud of smoke. When this clears, we find ourselves in a cave labeled **Headquarters of Mars.** Here three weird puppets go into their own gleeful dance and sing their song:)*

GODS OF WAR:

We're Immortal gods of war.
We are Wotan, Mars and Thor
And we love to see the humans
Play their games.
Once they used just sticks and stones.
Even then they piled up bones
But now they fight with lovely
Gorgeous flames.

(Another explosion and another smoke dissolve and the song is over. We cut back to our diplomats.

First Dip:
Gentlemen! It's treaty signing time.

Tough Dip:
Yeah, but not here. De little guy might be watchin.

Pansy Dip:
Oh righto. Rawther.

Second Dip:
What if he should see a treaty?

Tough Dip:
Den he'd know what was in 'em.

Dutch Dip:
Und den he vouldn't vant 'em.

Tough Dip:
Yeah. Den we'd be oughta work.

Dutch Dip:
Und dot's not diblomatic.

First Dip:
Gentlemen. Quiet please. Back to the embassies.

(They start marching toward us and the camera cuts back to Rip's crag. He is gone but Van Bummel is sitting there waiting for his return. Rip enters and says:)

Rip:
Derrick, where did you go?

Van B:
I told you, Rip, I'm powerless before such influences. The resistance must be yours. *(The music of the Diplomats' song is heard again)* They're coming back. One blow of your strong right arm will brush them into oblivion. Please Rip. *(Van Bummel again fades out of the scene as the diplomats enter)*

Tough Dip:
Hey, look! The guy woke up again. *(Rip advances menacingly. He raises his arm as if to strike but resolution fades. He looks behind him to see if Van Bummel is there or not. He isn't.)*

Rip:
Uh . . . Er . . . Where'd you get the silly looking outfits?

First Dip:
Well, it's like this. At the moment we're diplomats. International diplomats.

Pansy Dip:
Fascinating work, really. Amusing too at times.

Tough Dip:
Yeah. Good bowlin'. Fresh tunderbolts.
Rip:
What do you do?
First Dip:
Well, we uh . . .
2nd Dip:
What'd ya mean, what do we do?
First Dip:
It's really very simple. You see we . . .
4th Dip:
Why just last week we . . .
Tough Dip:
De guy's got a point. What do we do?
Pansy Dip:
Why sillies, we sign treaties.
All:
That's it. We sign treaties.
Rip:
Ah, who cares about such stuff. You know . . . It's funny . . .
(yawns) You folks always make me...sleepy.
Fourth Dip:
Ya Sleep iss de best. Easy now . . . Ve help you . . . So . . .
(They arrange him comfortably on his rocky couch and, again, go into their second slumber song)
SLUMBER SONG
Lulla, Lulla, Lullabye
We will isolate America from the sea to sea
We will guarantee the people white supremacy
We'll bring the country back again to normalcy
So Lulla Lullaby
*(As before, the scene fades out as the **Dwarfs** tiptoe off. The picture fades in again on the **Sleeping Rip.** Gradually the form of **Van Bummel,** now seated beside him, takes shape)*
Van B:
Rip, Rip, you great, stupid, well-meaning fool.
*(There is a moment of silence. **Rip** is still asleep. The music of "Happy Days Are Here Again" is heard. **Van Bummel** looks over his cliff.)*
Well, we're *all* coasting now—through the 20's—the bally-hoo years.

(We hear the cheers of a crowd)
**Does that bother you? It could be for Red Grange, Demp-
sey, or a matinee idol named Valentino.** *(The music builds
in tempo)* **Hold on now Van Winkle. Take a ride with stocks
and bonds. A ride on a dizzy market. A front seat on a rock-
eting, heart breaking roller coaster.**

*(The scene shifts to a stockmarket chart showing Dow-
Jones Averages during the 20's. The market line starts rising.
A rainbow appears. The line keeps reaching for a pot of gold
at its end)*

> **Steady Van Winkle. We're going up! It's '27. It's '28. Past
> Lindberg! Past Peaches Browning. Up! Up! Higher than a
> Wall Street broker's window. Look out, Van Winkle! We're
> at the peak!**

*(Crash! The chart line drops to the bottom. The picture shifts
again to **Van Bummel** and **Rip** on the mountain top. The
crash has startled **Rip** to his feet.)*

Van B:

> I thought that would wake you. But there's not much you
> can do about it just now. It's tough down there. Prosperity,
> they say, is just around the corner. There's the corner. *(He
> points over the ledge and we see a World War I veteran sell-
> ing apples on a street corner.)* **He'll make out. He'll get
> along somehow through '31 and '32. It's '33 now and new
> voices are heard in the world.** *(He turns out his hand and,
> miraculously, a **radio** appears on the ledge. He turns a dial
> and the face of the radio dissolves into the face of **Franklin
> D. Roosevelt** making his first inaugural address)*

F.D.R:

> My friends. This great nation will endure as it has
> endured—will revive and will prosper. Let me assert my
> firm belief that the only thing we have to fear is fear itself.
> *(Now we see our two mountaintop friends again. **Van Bum-
> mel** turns the dial)*

Van B:

> And in Germany there is a new chancellor. He's speaking
> at this very moment in the Reichstag. *(The **radio** dissolves
> into another news shot of 1933. This shows a wildly gestic-
> ulating **Hitler** and the sound track carries his frantic,
> screaming voice. When he has finished, his audience
> cheers and starts a swelling chorus of*

Deutchland, Deutchland uber alles. During **Hitler's** *speech the camera has cut back to* **Rip** *listening at the radio. He shows only amusement. His pointed finger circles his temple and he lies down again.* **Van Bummel** *pleads with him)* **Rip! Is there <u>nothing</u> that will keep you awake? That menacing chorus is now the rage. It's '36 and it's a hit in Austria.** *(We see a news film of* **Mussolini** *strutting with his raised fist.)* **It's '37—It reaches the Saar and the Rhineland.** *(Hitler is seen reviewing his troups.)* **'38—and it sounds in Munich.** *(Neville Chamberlain and Hitler are seen signing the Munich pact.)* **It's '39—It's September 2nd!** *(BOOM! We see a building fall.)* **That was Warsaw!** *(BOOM! Another building is bombed.)* **That was Paris.** *(BOOM!)* **Dunkirk!** *(We see British soldiers out to sea to their boats. BOOM!)* **Moscow!** *(BOOM!)* **Stalingrad!** *(BOOM!).* **PEARL HARBOR!** *(Rip has been only moderately aroused by the earlier explosions but now at the crash of Pearl Harbor he jumps to his feet.)*

Van B:

Are you awake now Van Winkle? Thank God. That means the end of this particular group of conquerors. *(They look down at the Earth and see American soldiers landing on South Pacific islands.)* **Listen!** *(The music is now "Praise the Lord and pass the ammunition.)* **It's their swan song.**

Rip:

They're hearing it in North Africa, Italy, France, Luzon, the Solomons.

54

Van B:
And now, praise God, in Germany. *(We see the treads of a tank roll over a burning swastika flag. Then we see and hear New York's Broadway in a great celebration.)*

Rip:
V.E. Day!! Hurray! It's as good as over. *(He starts to sit down.)*

Van B:
On your feet, Rip! Your real fight is just beginning.

Rip:
What do you mean? We've won the war—practically. Those few Japs still resisting can't touch America.

Van B:
Yes, the Japs will be taken care of. *(We see MacArthur striding through the surf on his return to the Philippines.)* But a world's problems are just beginning. They need you down there, Van Winkle.

Rip:
We've done our part. America is safe.

Van B:
You think so. Listen. *(He snaps on the radio.)*

Radio:
Ankana, July 30th. Tension mounted in the Balkans today. Russia has made three distinct moves to extend her sphere of influence westward. Turkey is feeling pressure from the same source in the matter of the Dardenelles.

Rip:
That's a long way off, Derrick.

Van B:
It's as close as your own back yard. Twelve and a half minutes by rocket. *(He turns the dial.)*

Radio:
Tienstin, China. August 1st. Fighting between the Communist and Nationalist forces continued in the border provinces today as peace talks were broken off abruptly in Nanking.

Rip:
You're getting farther and farther away.

Van B:
Listen, you fool!

Radio:

New York. August 15th. Dr. Theodore Koch, Dean of American scientists, today declared that biological warfare must become a part of America's armament. "We cannot" Dr. Koch said, "permit other nations to out-distance us in this field."

Van B:

Biological warefare. Germicidal warefare. Agricultural blight with starvation for a world. Another year and Hitler would have had them. Ten more years and ten sovereign nations will have them. Science can now destroy us. But not save us. We've got to turn to the philosophers—to the Teacher from Galilee—to the poets.

Rip:

Those dreamers?

Van B:

Yes, those dreamers. Jesus—"And men shall beat their swords into plowshares." Tennyson—"The Parliament of Man." There was a dreamer who, a century ago, foresaw to-day's dreadful Dilemma. (**Bummel** *takes a small book from his pocket. He opens this and hands it to his friend. We see two verses in print and* **Rip** *reads these aloud:*)

For I dipped into the future   Heard the heavens filled with shouting
Far as human eye could see.   And there rained a ghastly dew
Saw a vision of the world   From the nations 'airy navies
With all the wonders that would be.   Grappling in the central blue.

Van B:

Aerial warfare. This was written a hundred years ago remember. The destruction of half our civilization. And finally, Man's only salvation—a *Federation of the World.*

Rip:

But we're not ready for it.

Van B:

Of course we're not ready for it. But there's no other way out. It's either that or extinction.

Rip:

Okay, my Idealist. How about the Russians?

Van B:

It's our best answer to them.

Rip:

Hah! Some answer.

Van B:

Of course we've got to start with the democracies. And let it grow into world union. Tennyson's prophecy <u>will</u> come true. But shall that Federation of the World come only after a new dark age?

*(But now we hear the old, familiar music of the **Dwarfs**. The silly grin returns to **Rip's** face and he says:)*

Rip:

Why, here come my friends, the Dwarfs. They'll set me straight.

Van B:

They'll set you straight!! They'll lullaby you to sleep again. At least they'll try. Please, Rip. You're the American voter. Keep your eyes open.

*(**Van Bummel's** form fades out of the scene and **Rip** is alone on the mountain top. Then the scene changes to a stylized Capital Building in Washington and, during the vamp before the song, our six **Dwarfs** emerge. The four in the middle carry a sign reading SENATE COMMITTEE. In front and in back are two **Party Bosses**.)*

(As they march, they sing their:)

SENATOR'S SONG

We are legislative mentors,
We're habitual disenters,
With officers in Washington D.C.
And we have a lofty notion
That the great Atlantic ocean
Is the surest bet for saving liberty.

And we hold no brief for greetings
In the form of global meetings
For that only raises taxes in the end.
Why should anyone expect us
To give dough? They don't respect us.
If we're tough enough the world will be
our friend.

*(The six are now almost up to **Rip's** mountain top. They pause while each Party Boss sings a verse)*

1st Party Boss:

We're the big shot party wheels.
We train senators like seals
And we've brought along our troup
To do their act.
They can juggle, they can dance,
Sing soprano, they'll entrance
Any voters who are not concerned
with facts.

2nd Party Boss:

If they all were on our string
Then our troubles
Would take wing
And the people we could
Thoroughly distain
But too many keep remote
(That's the lump within our throat)
But here are some
We're sure will entertain.

(Now a Fourth-of July speaker's platform has, miraculously, appeared. The 1st Party Boss introduces each Senator who then goes into his rhythmic oration.)

The Senator from the East:

In this land of milk and honey
I represent the money
That is found above
The Mason-Dixon line
And I try to save my bosses
from pecuniary losses
By some methods that
I'd rather not divine.

The Senator from the West:

From the land of spurs and boots
And the sunkist citrus fruits
I found my way to Washington one day.
I'm as quiet *as a mouse*
When I'm in the Upper House
Speaking only when instructed
What to say.

The Senator from the South:

I'm a julep drinkin' boy
Filibusterin' is my joy
I'm the big wind from the South
Whoooo eeee!
I campaign on catfish dinners
With the poll tax, I'm a winner.
A vote don't count
Unless it's cast for me.

*(They come down from the platform and, to the vamp of the music, march onto **Rip's** ledge and group themselves around him. The music shifts into swing-time and **Rip** starts a musical dialogue with the Senators. He opens this with his song:)*

I'VE BEEN HEARIN' STUFF

Rip:

I been hearin' stuff that ain't too nice,
It scares me stiff, I need advice.
A friend says the world is shrunk up small.
There ain't no room for hidin' at all.
Now that ain't right. He's crazy in the head.
Say it an't so. I want to go to bed.

Senators:

Well look here Bud, why all this rukus?
We can help you out but we gotta have a cuckus.

(They caucus with a "huddle" dance routine.)

Rip:

He says one more war means we're done for good,
It'll put us right back where the cave man stood.
Must I stay awake for the world below?

Senators:

Let's ask the boss. The answer's—No.
Who cares for the world and all that fuss?
We're interested in the old U Us.
Forget about the French, the Czech and Greek
'Cause Europe's always up a creek.

Rip:

Now that's just what I wanted to hear.
Let's get some sleep. There's nothin to fear.

Senators:

Now you're talkin' Stop your fuss.
Close your eyes and listen to us.

*(They gently lower him into his favorite recumbent position
and go into their Slumber Song)*

Lulla, Lulla, Lullabye
We will wave the flag of sovereignty for you on high.
If it brings another war it's just your sons who'll die
We'll strike first another time and so you needn't sigh
So Lulla Lullabye

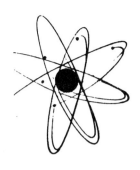

*(It's the same old routine. **Rip** is asleep. The **Dwarfs** tiptoe off as the scene fades out. Darkness for a while. And silence. But, no, it is not really silence. The faint whine of a great electric generator is growing in volume. Now mathematical formuli are writing themselves across our screen as on a great blackboard. Now they begin to spin and soon they merge into a great $E = MC^2$. Einstein's formula remains and over it and through it we see a montage that might be labelled "Science gone Mad." Test tubes, electrical monstrosities, industrial bowels. The whine has grown louder, ear splitting. Now from a whirling laboratory emerge atomic symbols—the little solar systems dear to the cartoonist's heart. They are moving toward the camera. Above the screaming din we hear **Van Bummel's** shout: RIP! In heaven's name wake up! RIP! There's no more time! The red center of an atom symbol fills the screen and—**BOOM!!** It is the Hiroshima explosion and we see the great mushroom cloud rise and swell. Darkness as the roar subsides. Then we see the mountain top. **Rip** and **Bummel** are on their faces. Slowly they rise and peer over the edge into the red hell of flame beneath them.)*

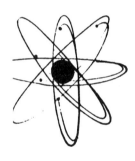

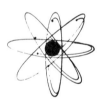

Rip:
Derrick. Oh Derrick, what was that?

Van Bummel:
An atom bomb. It's horrible. But you've got to look. The poets, Rip, did know best. "Man's inhumanity to man makes countless thousands mourn."

Rip:
And we can't stop wars. The little men told me so.

Van Bummel:
Listen Rip! *(In the red glow of flames beneath, he pleads with his frightened friend. It is his "Sermon-on-the-Mount" delivered with passion:)*

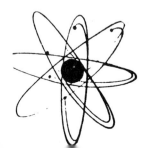

Van Bummel:

> They'll tell you that war is inevitable,
> That it's part of the nature of man,
> That the cycle is set and there's no use to fret
> And each peace just a twenty year span
> But they lie in their teeth
> We know underneath
> They're just clutching at status quo.
> They're old men past their prime
> Crying "Peace in our time"
> For their miserable few years to go.

*(The scene shifts to the **Wotan, Thor** and **Mars** group. They are delighted with all the flames and horror around them and go into a menacing chant:)*

> Hiroshima,
> Nagasaki,
> Watch the Japs go boom.
> San Francisco,
> Cincinnati,
> London, hear your doom.

*(The scene shifts back to **Van Bummel** who is still pleading with **Rip**.)*

Van Bummel:

> They'll tell you that man is competitive,
> That always he'll fight for his tribe
> And I'll say that they're right
> But the meaning of fight
> Doesn't have to include suicide.

(The Puppets continue their chant:)

Hiroshima
Nagasaki
Bummel thinks some bars
Will hold us in
He's full of gin,
We're Wotan, Thor and Mars.

Van Bummel:
  If you happen to come from Texas
  You'll be proud of that lone star state
  But you'll save some zeal
  For the commonweal
  Of our Nation—God keep her great.
  And while you can love your country
  And boast you're American
  You can still hold allegience to a world
  And make it an Eden for Man.

Mars etc.
  Hiroshima! Nagasaki!
  Wotan, Thor and Mars.
  Forget your qualms,
  With atom bombs
  Now we can crack the stars!

*(During this final chant, **Rip** has risen in righteous wrath.*
*He strides over to **Mars** and with one great blow strikes him*
down. The camera is now out in space and from there we
can see the evil spirits tumbling down, down, down. In
their fall they miss the Earth entirely and continue on into
*outer darkness. Now **Rip** opens the **Bummel** book and*
reads aloud the final verses:)

Rip:

*Then the war-drums beat no longer and the battle flags were furled
In the Parliment of Man, the Federation of the World.*

*There the common sense of most did hold a fretful world in awe
And the kindly earth did prosper lapped in universal law.*

*At long last, **Rip** is standing erect. Inspired. He looks up and
sees the Tennyson prophesy written bold across a blue sky,*

The End

Now three titles appear:

In the original story, Rip
only nodded off long enough
to miss the American Revolution.
We kept him up there in the
mountains right down to the
nuclear age.

The makers of this film,
members of the Todd School,
have bombarded him with the
great issue of Life and Death
on this planet and hereby
apologize for not including
any final solution.

We only wish we could.

*This title remains on the screen while **Rip's** voice is heard saying to us:*

*"**Our Dreadful Dilema"** to use Van Bummel's phrase, has no easy answer. The peril to our planet has been documented in chilling detail by Jonathan Schell and others. But all are vague on the solution. One point they agree on: It must be political, not military. Translated, this means **some** version of Tennyson's Parliment of Man. Yes, versions have been tried and found wanting. Wilson's League and our own U.N. have been disappointments. As **Rip** said "We're not ready for it." As **Van Bummel** answered "Of course we're not ready for it but there's no other way out. It's either that or extinction." Then he adds: "Tennyson's prophecy **will** come true but shall that Federation of the world come only after a New Dark Age?"*
*We wonder. What do **you** think?*

(Now a final title appears.)

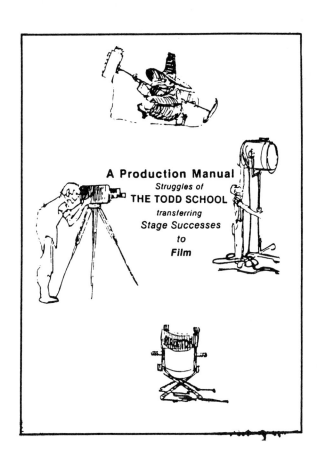

A Production Manual
Struggles of
THE TODD SCHOOL
transferring
Stage Successes
to
Film

A Production Manual
by Roger Hill

We are bombarded with questions on how this film was produced. An army of young moderns who now own video cameras hope to use these creatively. Many schools and most universities offer credit courses in "Cinema." Text books on the subject abound. This will not be another. Instead, it's a look into the long-ago when the Todd School, successful on the stage, attempted transfer of those successes to film. This meant synchronizing sound and picture. Hollywood had accomplished this in 1927 by use of a flexible cable tying the projector to a phonograph turnetable. We never managed this but our Physics teacher devised a stroboscopic system where a light on a disc would drift forward or back. Watching this, a practiced hand at the projector could vary its speed and approximate a lip-sync.

In 1927, *Vitaphone* revolutionized Hollywood when Al Jolson was heard as well as seen in *The Jazz Singer.* Sound had been added by phonograph. Its turntable was attached to the film projector by that cable. The system was crude and trouble prone and lasted only a year. I'm one of the few alive to remember the madness of that period: The projectionist was a harried man with multiple problems. He needed skill to start the picture and sound simultaneously and he needed luck to hold them together. The film could break or the needle could jump a groove. Either mishap would bring pandemonium. There would be boos and cat-calls lasting a minute or more until sync could be restored. Not until a new *optical* sound with its vibrations printed on the film itself did the "talkies" come of age.

"The Jazz Singer" was a film version of a story by Samson Raphaelson that had been published in the *Saturday Evening Post* ten years earlier. I was in on the birth of that story when "Raph" and I were in college together. I was a class ahead of him and slightly important as editor of the *Siren,* humor magazine of the University of Illinois at Champaign. My success in that job was largely due to his contributions. I was facinated and envious of his creative ability. He had a bureau drawer full of story manuscripts, including his poignant *Jazz Singer.* Each story had clipped-on rejection slips. These had come from all the magazines buying fiction back then: *Red-Book, McCall's, Sat-Eve-Post* and others. They prospered on short stories and serials before they died. *New Yorker,* the only magazine now buying fiction, had not been born.

Now back to the Todd School and our early efforts in cinema. We produced about 20 films with varying success. At least half are now preserved on video tape including a Drama League *Twelfth Night* directed by Orson Welles with costumes by Orson Welles and scenery by Orson Welles. It's the untold sequel to the oft-told story of how Orson failed with his Drama League Contest production of *Julius Caesar*. All books on Welles tell this tale. The shortest version is in a *New Yorker* Profile written by Russell Maloney. Here's an excerpt:

> Todd is an expensive preparatory school of considerable antiquity, now run on severely progressive lines. The present headmaster, Roger Hill, a slim, white-haired, tweed-bearing man, who looks as if he had been cast for his role by a motion-picture director, has never let the traditional preparatory-school curriculum stand in the way of creative work. All the boys spend as much time as they want in the machine shop, the printshop, the bookbindery, or the school theatre. Orson Welles was at Todd from 1926 to 1931. In those five years he completed eight years of academic work and qualified for admission to college, provided the college wasn't too particular about mathematics. Also abetted by the delighted Mr. Hill, he gave himself a thorough course in the fundamentals of the theatre. It is probable that Welles, as a boy, wore more crepe hair and putty noses than most actors do in a lifetime. When he was thirteen, he began directing the Todd Troupers, the school dramatic society. His first big job that year was a production of "Julius Ceasar," played in togas but nevertheless embodying many of the ideas he later used for the Mercury's "Caesar." This was the Todd School's entry in the annual Drama League contest for high schools and little-theatre groups around Chicago. It didn't get the prize; the judges explained that, meritorious as the production was, the two lads who played Cassius and Mark Antony were both too mature to be bona-fide students. This was a severe disappointment for Welles, who had cast himself in these two leading roles to make sure that they were played exactly right.

On leaving Todd, Orson spent a summer riding a donkey cart through Ireland trading sketches and paintings for lodging at night. He had graduated at 15 with a scholarship waiting for him at Harvard. Pictured here is his senior class picnic that June of 1931. Those *ledern hosen* had been acquired the summer before when, with another Todd boy, he had hiked through the Bavarian Alps to Munich where in a beer hall he watched a little rabble-rouser with a comic mustache flay the air with gestures and harangue an audience.

In Ireland, instead of returning home, he sent me this wire: HAVE A JOB AT THE GATE THEATRE AND SOME COURSES AT TRINITY COLLEGE. WIRE OBJECTIONS. He got the lead part of *Duke Karl Alexander* in *Jew Suss* and sent Hortense a self portrait. By Christmas he was offered a job in London but a Ministry of Labour regulation denied him the necessary work permit and he returned to Woodstock to direct our dramatics the second semester.

Peddling his paintings for food and lodging, an itinerant schoolboy wanders through Galway and the Aran Islands before ending up as an actor in Dublin. Here's a self-portrait he sent back to Hortense.

Victory at last in Chicago

In May he finally won the Drama League Cup for Todd. The conception of a huge "book" with pages opening to different scenes came from Kenneth Macgowan, the great innovator of that early day in Provincetown and in the movies. But Orson's painting for each scene was original.

Our daughter, Joanne at 16.

Todd had a few girls, all faculty daughters. Joanne, pictured above, played *Viola.* The twin brother, *Sebastian,* was played by our son, Rog. Shakespeare's twins are shipwrecked and thrown up on the beaches of a strange land. This is peopled with comedic characters indulging in much horse-play. The land, appropriately enough, is named *Illiria.* Orson's daughter spent a few years in our lower school and traveled with our *Bach to Boggie* musical group delighting audiences by belting out current hits such as *No business like show business.* In the *Rip* film she's one of the gremlins. If you want to identify her, she's in a blue hat atop the rum keg when the dwarfs are first seen. Today she's Chris Feder, successful author, writing text books for Scott-Foresman.

Our daughter, Joanne, at sixty-five. Still feisty and with arms often akimbo, this super teacher now faces the vicissitudes of retirement to that dubious status of Senior Citizen."

Her husband, Hascy Tarbox, an advertising executive, played Sir Andrew Aguecheeck, the simpering little knight loaded with money so coveted by his bibulous fat friend Sir Toby Belch.

Others in the Rip cast are now famous including the leads played by prep-school seniors: **Van Bummel** *by Jon Geis, now a Manhattan psychologist;* **Rip** *by Gahan Wilson, now a cartoonist of note.*

71

Twelfth Night was the final Todd production directed by Orson. The next year we made a film version but Welles was touring the country with **Katherine Cornell** and her three hit shows: *The Barretts of Wimpole Street, Candida* and *Romeo and Juliet.* Orson played Shakespeare's *Mercutio* and Shaw's poet, *Marchbanks.* Now he was famous although only 18. He had dropped out of school at 15. Remarkable? Not really. Most of the world's creators have been self taught. Shaw quit school at 14. Which reminds me that our boy was producing Shaw when only 12. We never traveled with that show but on a Todd stage he played the lead in *Androcles and the Lion,* the great agnostic's satiric put-down of the Christian Martyrs.

Later, in Mercury Theater days, the 23-year-old Orson with three shows running simultaneously on Broadway, phoned the 81-year-old Shaw and got permission to produce his *Heartbreak House.* In this he played the 88-year-old Captain Shotover and landed on the cover of *Time Magazine.*

TIME
The Weekly Newsmagazine

GEORGE ORSON WELLES
Volume XXXI   Number 19

A Marriage at Nineteen

Speaking of age and early maturity, during the Cornell tour we planned a summer theater festival at Todd complete with the Irish stars from Dublin's Gate Theatre and a campus full of "students" paying money for the privilege of acting bit parts at night and slaving on scenery and costumes all day. At the end of that summer Orson married the most beautiful of his students, Virginia Nicolson. They went to New York; he got jobs on the Radio; the rest is history.

But before the marriage there was that Theater Festival. It was 1934 and we had the presumption to compete with a great World's Fair in Chicago. That **"Century of Progress"** was immensely popular and was the first World's Fair ever to turn a profit. It's enticements stretched for miles along the shore of Lake Michigan. We had brought the Irish stars over from Dublin and what saved us from financial disaster was snob appeal. Society leaders became our sponsors and the Social Register our mailing list. This brought scads of overblown copy on the society pages. *Marshal Field's* ran full page ads featuring gowns suitable for Woodstock openings. We shamelessly courted the society editors sending one of our sleeper busses to bring them to opening nights. A man of impeccable social standing was aboard to serve drinks enroute. On the way back he provided them with typewriters for their fables; always a paragraph on the gown worn by Hortense Hill although it probably came from Sears Roebuck.

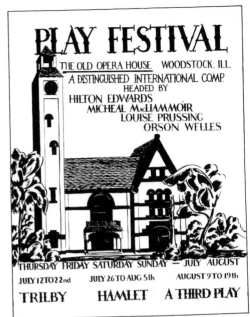

PLAY FESTIVAL

THE OLD OPERA HOUSE   WOODSTOCK, ILL.
A DISTINGUISHED INTERNATIONAL COMP.
HEADED BY
HILTON EDWARDS
MICHEAL MacLIAMMÓIR
LOUISE PRUSSING
ORSON WELLES

THURSDAY FRIDAY SATURDAY SUNDAY — JULY AUGUST

JULY 12 TO 22nd   JULY 26 TO AUG. 5th   AUGUST 9 TO 19th

TRILBY   HAMLET   A THIRD PLAY

Acutually, Horty was a harried gal, not only on openings but every night of that wild summer. This note appeared on every program:

A buffet supper with the cast will be served on the campus of the Todd School after the performance. Reservations are necessary and these may be made at the box office any time before the close of the first intermission.

Those suppers were gala events under flood lights on a patio between two dormitory buildings. Lasting for hours, they were nightclub experiences. Our own cast, all exhibitionists, would start things off but the ball would be picked up by celebrity guests. Hedda Hopper sang and DeWolf Hopper did his lifetime specialty act, a super-sad rendition of *Casey at the Bat.* We were his final audience. He died the next week. Horty divided her time between hosting her guests and persuading her temperamental cooks to stick it out for the season. Also gulping coffee to fortify herself for gushing "good-nights" before taking up her now-until-dawn chore of preserving the virginity of twenty nubile females placed in her care by trustful mothers.

Here is Orson's 1934 purple prose that headed the literature we mailed to every wealthy family on Chicago's North Shore.

Like a wax flower under a bell of glass, in the paisley and gingham county of McHenry is Woodstock, grand capital of mid-Victorianism in the Midwest. Towering over a Square full of Civil War monuments, a band stand and a spring house is the edifice in the picture. This very rustic and rusticated thing is a municipal office building, a public library, a fire department and, what is more to our purpose, an honest-to-horsehair Opera House.

This was resented by the citizens of a growing little "city" proud of its Woodstock Typewriter factory and huge Alemeite plant. Today the town glories in its unique charm. Americans from every state are drawn to its antique shops, its restaurants and its Opera House, now designated a National Monument. Its restoration, with fire department and city offices removed, cost nearly a million. Its stage, now permanently alive under Doug Rankin, is hallowed not only by the ghost of Orson Welles but of other great names who followed: dozens of young students from the Goodman and DePaul including Paul Newman, Geraldine Page, Shelly Berman, Betsy Palmer, Sam Wanamaker. Midwestern towns are full of "Squares" but each is crowded with a Courthouse and other buildings that negate charm. Woodstock's tree-filled park is the one pure gem.

The McHenry County Courthouse and Jail, on the other side of the Square was built in 1857. It now holds antique shops and a fine restaurant. Your menu will be headed by Orson's prose which was so resented when we first used it in our Festival promotion. One of the restaurant rooms is a jail cell. Eugene Debs, the great orator and perpetual candidate for President on the Socialist ticket was confined there. This for his part in the Pullman strike of 1894. The famous Clarence Darrow was defense lawyer.

We did three plays: *Trilby* with Orson's demonic *Svengali.* Then *Tsar Paul* to show off Hilton Edward's recent European triumph and the *Hamlet* that had made Michael MacLiammoir famous. The *New York Times* sent Brooks Atkinson to cover that important event.

Here's our Act V tableaux just before the bodies start piling up from the envenomed foil and poisoned cup. Above Micheal is Louise Prussing, leading lady for Leslie Howard until his death. At the top of the pyramid is Orson playing the wicked uncle, Claudius, the King.

A little later, when Hamlet is horizontal, the tag line that everyone knows is spoken by his faithful friend, *Horatio*

> **Good night, sweet prince;**
> **And flights of angels**
> **Sing thee to thy rest.**

Our *Horatio*, that summer was Charles, "Blacky," O'Neal, grandfather of Tatum O'Neal, the child prodigy and Academy Award winner in *Paper Moon.* Blacky's wife, Constance Heron, was our *Ophelia.*

Thornton Wilder, a lifetime Hamlet scholar, lived in our home during the weeks of rehearsal on this play. The *Todd Press* had just started printing our Shakespeare books and he was amazed at the machinery he found operating on the campus. The text books with their amazingly long life and record-breaking sales are the product of Welles more than Hill so I can indulge in some boasting. Todd had established the printing plant and the publishing company for some books, far less glamorous, I had written earlier. When my amazing pupil began designing sets and costumes for our Shakespeare shows. I conceived the idea of putting his sketches and stage directions in book form for the use of other schools. I wrote the Introductory chapters and these were coming off the press when Thornton visited our shop. I had asked Orson to finish up this section with a chapter on the Elizabethan theater. When Thornton read the first three sentences he pronounced them the finest thumbnail summation of Shakespeare's genius ever written. Here they are:

> **Shakespeare said everything. Brain to belly; every mood and minute of a man's season. His language is starlight and fireflies and the sun and moon. He wrote it with tears and blood and beer and his words march like heart-beats.**

It was stunning prose. Now consider the boy's art work. He was 16 when he made the drawings for our books. He was 22 when his Broadway production of Shakespeare's *Caesar* was the talk of America. It was the Mercury Theater's first offering. The date was 1937, two years before Hitler's attack on Poland which started World War II. Mussolini with his clenched fist and jutting jaw had founded Fascism. In Germany Hitler was outdoing him in race hatred. His goose-stepping Brownshirts were dominating our news. Orson dressed Shakespeare's vainglorious Caesar and his cohorts in Nazi-like uniforms and put the impractical Brutus in a blue serge suit. The analogy to current events was perfect. It was played on a bare and blackened stage with no scenery. Stunning effects were produced by lights.

One such effect that drew gasps from the audience and raves from the reviewers was at the end of Antony's funeral oration. His rebuttal of Brutus begins in front of angry and hostile listeners. Then with cunning and wile and superb dramatics he lures them away from soft-spoken reasonableness and substitutes anger and passion and hate. His final call to *RISE* and *MUTINY* was made with out-stretched arms silhoutted against a sky. As a 16-year-old, Orson had planned this scene and drawn a picture to show how torch lights could accomplish the effect.

Our first book included three plays: *Caesar*, *The Merchant of Venice* and *Twelfth Night*. Here is the boy's illustration for one of the Casket Scenes in *The Merchant*.

ACT II Scene I
BELMONT—Portia's House

(Portia is receiving a suitor, the Prince of Morocco. He strikes a pose and waits for Portia to say something. She doesn't. He strikes another pose, but still gets no response. Finally he raises one hand dramatically and delivers a speech.)

     Morocco: **Mislike me not for my complexion,**
               The shadowed livery of the burnished sun,
               To whom I am a neighbour and near bred.

For *Twelfth Night* I'll show just the boy's sketch for the end of Scene III in Act I.

Sir Toby: **Let me see thee caper:** *(He cracks his whip at his friend who bounds out of the way.)*

Sir Toby: **Ha! higher** *(He cracks his whip another time. The little man prances out of the way, half frightened, half showing off.)*

'he fat Sir Toby Belch
'ith his simpering
ttle friend, Sir Andrew
\guecheek, have several
ilarious drinking scenes.

Sir Toby: **Ha, Ha! Excellent!** *(Roaring with laughter, they bound about in a circle and off.)*

(CURTAIN)

THE MERCURY
Shakespeare

Edited for READING *and*
Arranged for STAGING *by*

Orson Welles and Roger Hill

Julius Caesar
The Merchant of Venice
Twelfth Night

Published by HARPER & BROTHERS
New York *and* London

Those first three Shakespeare plays were published in 1934 by The Todd Press. When critics gave us good reviews, Chicago's *Krock & Brentano* store filled its Wabash Avenue window with a special display including originals of the Welles drawings. This brought publishers with offers. We chose Harpers for its prestige and also its willingness to let our school shop continue the manufacture. It was a foolish choice. Harper & Brothers had no sales force calling on schools as did Scott-Foresman and McGraw-Hill. But luck was with us. Harpers soon sold their school business to McGraw-Hill and this aggressive outfit carried on for forty years.

Our complete print shop also had its bindery with folding machines and other necessary noise-makers.

No other school texts have ever approached that record of longevity. School boards have a fixation. They insist on **new** copyright dates. Our books were a notable exception. After closing a yacht-charter business in the Caribbean we returned to our native Midwest and found, in Rockford, Illinois, great-grandchildren studying their highschool Shakespeare from books copyrighted fifty years earlier. *Wow!*

Now I'm thinking of an edition of these first three plays in a new form and for a new clientele consisting of adults. Actually, our first sales in Chicago were to adult readers. Then school publishers came to us with attractive wholesale offers. The idea now is to offer a Shakespeare package for the educated public. It would be a plastic box with a hinged lid and have a spine duplicating an antique book so it could sit handsomely on the shelf of a home library. Inside it would contain the printed plays plus three cassette tapes. The sound on each of these would be the Welles voice reading a play and commenting on it. Then his discussion of Elizabethan times in general and the Bard in paticular. I've told you what Thornton Wilder said about Orson's written comments. Students who have listened to his lectures will attest they are equally inspiring. This plan will insure their preservation.

Twelfth Night, in 1932, was the last Todd play that Orson directed. He had returned from Ireland and with it won that elusive Drama League cup in Chicago. It was planned for our graduation program. In those June affairs we used no imported speaker with predictable platitudes. Instead we would give our audience a day of entertainment including a senior play.

When Orson left for his two year tour with Katharine Cornell we wrote for our seniors a riotous opera in rag time called *The Judgment of Paris.* It had a college setting and an *Iliad* plot. A wierdo little professor of Greek has hots for the beauty queen and is knocked cold by her boy friend, the football captain. The pipsqueak dreams he is Paris, the Prince of Troy who was abandoned by his mother, Hecuba, because she learned he would bring trouble to her land. Raised by shepherds, he became the perfection of youthful masculine beauty and was given the job of choosing which goddess, *Juno, Venus,* or *Minerva* should receive a golden apple. All three offered bribes. He chose *Venus* when she promised him the most beautiful woman in the world, *Helen.* This meant stealing her from her husband, *Menelaus,* the Greek king. This started the Trojan War and, as Doctor Faustus put it, *launched a thousand ships.* In our play it launched two big war canoes. Here's our stage sea-scene with rows of oscillating waves and a trap door for *Neptune's* entrance. Of course the two boats were in a chase and never seen together on the stage. The picture here is just a publicity shot.

In production, Paris came first. He was paddling his new female who by now had begun to pall. His aria, before being stopped by *Neptune,* who rises out of the sea, includes these lines:

Oh Jove look down from up on high
And tell me frankly what's a guy
To do with this here ham-on-rye
Who thinks she's Peaches Browning.

(You'll have to be in retirement, or close to it, to remember the once notorious Peaches Browning.)   When the singing duo asks the Sea-God for directions his rythmic repy is

Troy?... Now... Let me see...
Second red light, hard-a-lee...
Why, brother, you can't miss it.

Paris paddles off and the Greeks, in hot pursuit, paddle on to have their singing session with *Neptune.* The Sea-God sinks beneath the waves and the war canoe is moving off stage as the curtain closes on the second act. Then curtain-calls and bows by the watery group.

Seniors would get diplomas shortly after their performance. Some will tell you they still had grease paint on their faces. Tarbox graduated two years after Welles. Here's his impression of an off-beat Headmaster handing out diplomas and maybe a little advice.

We filmed the stage play silently. Also recorded a sound track to dub on later. This "Dubbing" process is more difficult than recording the sound first and "Mugging" to it as the camera rolls. But dubbing **can** be done successfully. Witness all those commercial films distributed in different languages. You must do this in short segments and with much practice. If you're working with film you make continuous-playing loops for this. If your show is on tape you can dub short segments over and over. You'll automatically erase earlier mistakes.

For our "Todd Troupers" to meet stage professionals, both performers and directors, we would send a bus to Chicago and bring "Equity" folks out for a relaxing day in our suburb. Here we're showing one of our films to the cast of *Meet the People.* That's a very young *Nanette Fabray* wiping tears of laughter from her eyes.

Samson Raphaelson

1896 ▆▆▆▆▆▆▆▆▆▆▆▆▆▆▆▆▆ 1983

See last paragraph, first page of this supplement.

The friend I so idolized is now dead! With heavy heart I write this fact on a day that obituary columns recount his fame. This from his theater successes, his movie triumphs and his prize-winning short story collections. They fail to recount his teaching triumphs and his student's devotion. In the forties he taught creative writing at Illinois to a now-aging group of successful authors. Until yesterday when he died at home in his sleep, he was the favorite faculty member at Columbia. Devotion, and yes, *Love* are necessary words when describing his response from students. A book, which could be a best seller, will surely tell this story soon. May that biographer be adequate. I'll dig into my files to help. Wonderful letters from a wonderful man. I'll dig into memory for anecdotes, tales such as the *Lambkins Society* we founded for student playwrights, actors, composers and Thespians. This was mainly to design our own show-off insignia, a gold key engraved with the classic drama masks. Six feet away, however, a dead ringer for that proud pendant of Phi Beta Kappa.

*   *   *   *   *

I pause in front of my battered old portable and ponder: Should that last phrase be changed? Certainly the term, show-off. There were plenty of these in our group including me. Not Raph, however. He was the most talented and also the most modest. It was Po Field, I think, who came up with the idea of that deceptive insignia. Po was the son of Eugene Field , author of *Wynken, Blynken, and Nod* plus a hundred other classics for children. The great poet had nicknamed this son, *Posey.* The abbreviation stayed with him through his long career in advertising. Another in our group, Ed Morrissey, grew rich in that devious profession. In college, we were partners in a minor scam that kept us campus-rich. Ed drew cartoons and I whittled wheezes for the *Campus Scout,* a column in the *Daily Illini.* We published these in a thin book that sold well. Morrissey lived in Champaign and recently a relative presented a copy of *Boneyard Babblings* to the Alumni Association and they ran a story in their magazine. It included a jingle of mine in praise of a Champaign haberdasher who was generous with his credit. One couplet went

If 'twer not for thy charged up mercantile
I'd trod the campus wearing but a smile

Ed's illustration of the author was apt; a skinny kid, pencil on his ear, no worries on his mind, a grin for life's vicissitudes.

Ed Morrissey

1894 ▆▆▆▆▆▆▆▆▆▆▆▆▆ 1949

The cartoonist, too, is dead. Of that long-ago group, one pencil-pusher remains. Dubious distinction.

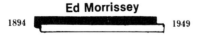

THE RIP FILM
★ ★ ★
Details of Its Production

Notice the huge old kleig lights, carbon-arc devices now obsolete.

This supplement grows overlong. It was planned as a few production notes o the Rip film. Instead, I've delved into the history of a school, famous for stag productions, struggling to transfer these to film. Now a publishing deadlin looms. This book must go to press. I'll close it with a picture of one Rip scen and other contents of an old file on this film. The folder is covered with dust an thick with lists. These include the necessary sets and props and costumes. Eac item is followed by its expected cost. In other words, a **Budget**. This is a must you hope to work at all professionally.

Our costumes included a few that could be rented but there were **forty** tha had to be designed and made. This because each of the eight Gremlins wer through four or more transformations. They became senators, diplomats, an wierdo characters out of ancient history. Hascy Tarbox painted all forty. Here ar a few in reduced black and white.

Attila

Ghengis Kahn

Stout Cortes

In Washington Irving's story the little men on his mountain-top were the ghosts of sailors from Hendrick Hudson's ship, the *Half Moon.* That Dutch explorer had, in 1609, gone up the great river making his third inland trip desperately trying to find a route to the Indies. When near the site of Albany his crew mutinied and murdered him. Irving wrote his fantasy 200 years later. He made Hudson's crew into dwarfted villians living on a mountain-top drinking their brew and bowling their nine-pins. This caused the world's thunder.

Mountain Gnome

Flapper of the 1920's

Modern Diplomat

Senator from the South   **Political Boss**

Our allegory uses Irving's characters, his plot and his opening sentence, "Whoever has made a voyage up the Hudson must remember the Katskill mountains". Then he describes the dejected, henpecked Rip in the village below and hands us our opening song by writing: "Rip would console himself, when driven from home, by frequenting a club of philosophers and sages of the village. These held their sessions on a bench before a small inn."

Finally he has Rip go squirrel hunting up in the mountains. This to avoid that termagant wife. On the summit he meets the little men with their keg of brew, the contents of which put him to sleep for twenty years. Here our allegory parts company with Irving. The next-to-closing title reads: *In the original story,* **Rip only nodded off long enough to miss the American Revolution. We kept him up there in the mountains right down to the nuclear age.**

Special Effects

Some of these may amaze you. Most were tricks taught us by Welles. He was busy in Hollywood then but managed two quick trips to Woodstock while his daughter, Chrissy, was playing one of the little Gremlins. To show a Senate Committee marching out of our Capitol, he had us paint the Washington building on beaverboard close to the camera and have actors do their march on a platform far away. The platform must be just below camera range while the feet are seen. To get the required depth of focus, an outdoor shot on a sunny day is needed. In the same way we show diplomats marching out of a castle and up into the mountains. As for mountain-climbing shots, a large gravel pit and trick camera angles accomplished the effects. Instant transformations of little Gnomes into villains out of history were simple lap-dissolves. Actors in the midst of blazing atomic fire was just double exposure.

By the time this film was made, sync was no longer a problem. We had motor-driven cameras and a matching sound-on-film recorder. A clapboard slap identified a frame and a visable jiggle identified its matching sound. Were our troubles over? Ha! That advantage brought as many problems as it solved. Silence on the set became necessary when the camera rolled. Including silence from the camera itself. It had to be "blimped". Enclosed. Microphones had to be held near each actor but out of camera range. Our play called for almost continuous songs and our "stage", a gymnasium, lacked the proper acoustics. The obvious answer to these multiple problems was to record all the sound in advance and have the actors "mug" the entire play. This was a necessity for the eleven-year-old Gremlins speaking many difficult dialects. It was a time-saver and a convenience for other members of the cast.

You too, with your modern video cameras, have eliminated the problem of syncronizing sound and picture but only at the expense of guality. It's simple to turn out pictures that may have great family value for future generations but without extra equipment and **copius editing** you have little hope of professionalism. In my dotage I own the latest in video cameras and accessories. This mainly for the use of grandchildren and great-grandchildren now in college. We've found that editing is enhanced and simplified by the help of a super-8, magnetic striped camera and projector. Not as expensive as it sounds. Video competition has plummeted Kodak movie sales. You can buy a camera and projector at one-third list price.

Benediction

Obviously, I am far too old to advise you on video technique. Professional studios now do amazing feats in editing but only at fantastic prices. This is to be expected because they have fantastic equipment and their control rooms look like those at Three-Mile-Island. But help and advice is available at reasonable prices in most large cities. Chicago, for instance, has classes all over town and for every need. The Art Institute has many courses which they will explain. Or a phone call to Chicago's *Center for New Television* on Hubbard Street will bring you a brochure telling of their "Workshops". The number to call is (312) 565-1787. Anyway, attend some classes somewhere and go to it. Who knows, you may turn out a masterpiece! Good luck.